The Modern Mom's Guide to a Calm and Healthy Home Birth in a Hectic World!

BORN AT Home

ALEJANDRA ALVAREZ

Copyrighted Material

BORN AT HOME: *A Modern Mom's Guide to a Calm and Healthy Home Birth in a Hectic World!*

Copyright © 2019 by Bella Bach Publishing. All Rights Reserved.

ISBN: 978-1-7334982-0-3

Editing by: Delgar Publishing
Cover and Interior design: Charles Bennett Graphic Design

Printed in the United States of America. ALL RIGHTS RESERVED

No part of this publication may be reproduced, stored in a retrieval system or transmitted in any form or by any means, electronic, mechanical, photocopying, recording, scanning or otherwise, except as permitted under Sections 107 or 108 of the 1976 United States Copyright Act, without either the prior written permission of the Publisher. For information about this title or to order other books and/or electronic media, contact the publisher: Bellabach Publisher, PMB #182 145 E. Sunset Rd. El Paso, TX 79922.

Limit of Liability/Disclaimer of Warranty: While the publisher and author have used their best efforts in preparing this book, they make no representations or warranties with respect to the accuracy or completeness of the contents of this book and specifically disclaim any implied guarantees. The advice and strategies contained herein are not suitable for every individual. You should consult with a professional as it concerns your specific situation. Neither the publisher nor author shall be liable for any outcome included but not limited to special, incidental, consequential, or other damages.

Table of Contents

Dedication v

Acknowledgment vi

Preface vii

Chapter 1
Why Home Birth? 1

Chapter 2
Finding the Right Midwife 17

Chapter 3
My First Home Birth 37

Chapter 4
The Silent Birth Secret 51

Chapter 5
My Second Home Birth 59

Chapter 6
Umbilical Cord 75

Chapter 7
My Third Birth 87

Chapter 8
Oh, What A Sacrifice! 101

Chapter 9
My Swan Song 113

CONCLUSION 129

APPENDIX 133

Dedication

This book is dedicated entirely to my wonderful husband, José. When I was pregnant with our first child, you challenged me by asking me whether it might be best to deliver our baby at home, rather than in a hospital. Little did I know that your question would serve as the inspiration to set me on a mission to learn what I now know about Home Births. Throughout my journey, you remained my loudest encourager and my most steady source of support. Thanks my love!

Acknowledgment

With the delivery of her first baby, Alejandra changed the way I had previously viewed birth. With only a flashlight and faint whispering, she demanded that her baby be born into a tranquil environment. She knew what she wanted and how to create the right atmosphere.

I loved her book, and I highly recommend it to anyone wanting to learn more about natural child birth.

Mary Darling (Alejandra's Midwife)

Preface

When I was pregnant with my first child, I had every intention of delivering my baby the way most people do — in a hospital. At the time, I sought out a doctor and a hospital that would assist me with the prenatal, delivery, and postpartum care of my baby in the safest and most peaceful manner possible. But the more I did my search for the most ideal arrangement to accommodate my wishes, the more I began to be concerned about what I was discovering with traditional childbirth methods. This book came about as a result of the alternative childbirth option I stumbled upon in the process of my search for the safest way to have my baby.

As stated earlier, I was certain that I was going to pursue the road traveled by most people and give birth to my baby in a hospital setting. But then my husband, who is a doctor himself, threw a wrench in my plans by asking me if I was 100% sure I wanted to go that route? So, when he asked me whether I was open to delivering our baby at home, I really did not know how to respond because I did not even know what the process entailed. Moreover, I didn't even know that it was possible to give birth at home. Up until the point of his question, I had never even considered bringing our child into the world any other way but in a hospital. Needless to say, his question got my thoughts to percolating.

In 2009, my search would come to an end. For in that year, I saw a documentary on the topic of home births titled "The Business of Being Born" by Ricky Lake. This exposé opened my eyes wide, and it changed my perspective forever regarding the overall child birth industry. The documentary discussed in great detail the truth about what really happens when a woman delivers her baby in a hospital. And believe me, you will be shocked by what it reveals. It also sheds light on the topic of home births, highlighting some of the experiences women go through while delivering their babies at home. In the end, I was totally convinced that I would not dare put the life of my child in the hands of an indifferent and profit-driven hospital system. Instead, the home birth option soon became my delivery method of choice.

This book is autobiographical in nature. In it, I attempt to educate readers about the world of home birthing by recounting my own natural childbirth experiences. Having successfully delivered all four of my children from the comforts of home, I feel that I am uniquely qualified to weigh-in and provide useful insights on this particular topic. Given the fact that each of my deliveries presented different challenges, I will use each birth as an individual case study to highlight the twists and turns that can occur and how a highly trained midwife can address them all.

Chapter One
WHY HOME BIRTH?

The reality is that nowadays women from all racial and socio-economic backgrounds are choosing to deliver their babies at home. Perhaps the biggest plus for expecting mothers who decide to home birth is that they will be in a comfortable environment around people they know. Additionally, all appointments and communications with healthcare providers and the attending midwife will also take place from the comforts of home. You will be in your room, on your bed, and surrounded by your things. There truly is no place like home! And that phrase carries so much more meaning when it comes to delivering a baby at home.

I know firsthand the many benefits of the home birth option, as I have experienced three of my own. Although each experience was uniquely different, they were all successful deliveries, nonetheless. As I write this particular chapter, I am currently going through the at home birth process for a fourth time with the same midwife I have had for all three of my previous pregnancies, and I'm due to give birth any day now. Yippee! Giving birth to all three of my children from the comfort of my home was so rewarding for me and my babies.

In this particular chapter, I would like to highlight a few of the benefits that make home births a more preferred option over the traditional healthcare industry methods, so much so that women from all walks of life are pursuing natural child birth in ever increasing numbers.

The Personal Attention

Whether this is your first baby, or perhaps even your second or third, know that the benefits of bringing a baby into the world from the comforts of home are endless. One of the main benefits you will enjoy is a more personalized level of care from your midwife. Most expecting moms desire a more one-on-one experience with their caregivers, but in the traditional hospital setting, such personalized attention to a single patient is typically not possible. On the other hand, the personal touch is one of the primary advantages of a home birth that makes the experience so appealing to mothers. Having your baby at home essentially puts you in the driver's seat versus the disempowered position mothers find themselves in with traditional birthing

> "One of the main benefits you will enjoy is a more personalized level of care from your midwife."

methods. Midwives are attentive to your needs throughout the entire pregnancy and also during your postpartum recovery. It is important to reemphasize that all the care you receive from them will be in the convenience and comfort of your own home.

Ability to Control The Process

A home birth will give you the ability to control the way you want the entire pregnancy process to go. Working in tandem with your midwife, you will develop a birth plan that, once followed according to YOUR wishes, will ensure the safe and successful delivery of your baby. I have personally seen where mothers will develop a birth plan and then events will happen completely the opposite of what they had intended, all because they failed to follow what they had mapped out. If all of your previous pregnancies have been without complications, then there is a great chance you will have a very smooth and successful home birth. With a home birth, you are able to control both the type and amount of distractions which are so rampant in hospitals settings.

> "A HOME BIRTH WILL GIVE YOU the ability to control the way you want the entire pregnancy process to go."

Additionally, you, as the mother, can avoid having to experience the inconveniences of all the technology involved with the conventional hospital birthing methods, which have never been medically proven to be safer for mothers than

God's tried and true method of natural birth. Scientific studies suggest that all of the latest gadgets and instruments do not decrease the number of intra-uterine fetal deaths or intrapartum deaths as compared to the number of babies that die during natural child birth. So, why the heavy reliance on technology if it is proven to yield no improvement in the rate at which mothers successfully deliver healthy babies as compared to at home births? Could it be a ploy used by the healthcare industry to justify the astronomical dollar amounts involved in the delivery of just one baby? I think so!

> "**You must take responsibility** for your own pregnancy and how you choose to bring your baby into the world."

Putting your pregnancy in the hands of the latest technologies or the most experienced physicians cannot guarantee that your hospital birth will be any safer than your carefully planned home birth. You must take responsibility for your own pregnancy and how you choose to bring your baby into the world. You alone are the only one who should make the decision whether or not to have all sorts of wires connected to you and your baby during pregnancy, or not. Keep in mind that technology can be a good thing, but it can also be simply just a bad thing.

Non-Hospital Environment

In a hospital environment, you will have constant

Why Home Birth?

interruptions of all sorts — mainly from the steady flow of doctors, nurses, and various other hospital staff members there to monitor your pregnancy situation. During labor, you will also be attached to a bevy of monitors to record every vital sign imaginable, from baby's movements to the intensity of mother's labor pains. While they are there to ensure your safety, they no doubt are intrusive and uncomfortable. Being confined to a bed with all sorts of monitors strapped to me, in addition to not having the freedom to eat and drink anything at all, was one of the main reasons I chose to have a home birth. That setup sounded to me like complete torture. This is not how we should be birthing our babies. With a home birth, you have the freedom to move around during your labor, as well as eat and drink if you wish to do so. And get this! You are even able to have your family in the same room if you wish to have them present during the delivery process.

> **"WITH A HOME BIRTH, YOU HAVE** the freedom to move around during your labor, as well as eat and drink if you wish to do so."

Conversely, delivering your baby in a hospital will greatly reduce the number of people you are permitted to have in the delivery room. It is important to point out that if you wish to have a single caregiver throughout the duration of your pregnancy, delivery, and post-partum recovery, a home birth will allow you to enjoy the close bond you form with a single midwife, from start to finish. Compare this to giving birth in a hospital where if the doctor is not available, hospital administrators will assign a different, unfamiliar doctor to care for you. Even worse, you could be attended to by multiple caregivers if the facility at which you happen to be having your baby is a partnership comprised of numerous physicians.

The reality is that if you choose to give birth at a hospital, you must bring your baby into the world on their terms. It ceases being about YOU and immediately becomes all about the hospital's bottom-line needs and desires. The truth is that doctors and nurses are like any of us. They too desire to leave work behind to be home by a certain time. Therefore, they will do what is most expedient to speed up your delivery. Think about this! Your baby may even desire to make its grand entry at a time when the hospital is experiencing a bed shortage, further hastening their need to get you in and out in a hurry. Speeding up the delivery process due to space availability challenges is one of the factors that often motivate doctors to perform unnecessary emergency cesarean procedures, rather than allowing the natural childbirth processes to play out. Inducing labor is always unnecessary unless there occurs an emergency with your baby or when your water breaks.

> **"THE REALITY IS THAT IF YOU CHOOSE** to give birth at a hospital, you must bring your baby into the world on their terms."

On the other hand, you will have the ability to maintain control and be able to make all your own decisions with a natural, home birth. This is where you have the opportunity to be in complete control of how you want your labor and delivery to go. I did not want anyone else making decisions

> **"YOU ARE IN THE DRIVER'S seat with a home birth."**

for me or forcing me to do something I did not want to do. If you want a nice, quiet, calm labor and delivery with only a few people around, or you wish something completely opposite, that is totally up to you. You are in the driver's seat with a home birth.

With conventional childbirth, you arrive ready to deliver, and they are ready with the drugs and monitors. Once you are in the delivery room, the clock starts ticking for the baby to come out. If the baby is not out by a certain time, then a normal delivery turns into a cesarean operation to bring your baby into the world. This unfortunate reality is what put me on edge with the hospital option. I had to do some research on this, and I discovered that cesarean deliveries are up significantly in the United States, and the number of them performed only increases during the holidays and in the evening hours when doctors want to be home before dinner time. During the holidays, doctor will typically leave you under the care of someone else so that they can take their vacations. I have witnessed this state of affairs to be so with many of my family members — that all of a sudden they are assigned to someone else while their doctor is away on vacation. In many cases, moms are informed of her primary caregiver change with as little as a days notice, or in some instances, she finds out about the change only after arriving at the hospital to deliver her baby.

My Experience

Initially, deciding to have a home birth was not a choice I arrived at easily. When I discovered that I was pregnant with my first baby, I was immediately overwhelmed by the weight of that news. At first, it was difficult for the information to sink in. However, when I saw my baby on the sonogram for the first time and when I heard its little heartbeat, it all became clear to me. The life of a precious baby was growing inside me, and it depended on the choices I made to ensure not only its survival but also its health and wellbeing. If you have ever been pregnant, then you can relate. But no sooner had I embraced the profound joy I felt regarding that first pregnancy, then my attention quickly shifted to the type of delivery I should pursue in order to bring my baby into the world.

By now, as an expecting mom, you have already heard it all from your family and friends…what they went through during their pregnancies and the complications of their deliveries. Sometimes they might say things that put you on edge, leaving you worried about how it will go for you. One bit of advice I would like to leave you with is that you should not pay too much attention to the war stories others tell you about

> **"With conventional childbirth, you arrive ready to deliver, and they are ready with the drugs and monitors. Once you are in the delivery room, the clock starts ticking for the baby to come out."**

their pregnancies because every expecting mom's situation is different. I caution you to simply listen to what they say, but don't accept that their situation will be yours. I have had three home births, and each of them was different in every way imaginable.

In the beginning with my first pregnancy, the only thing I knew for certain was that I wanted to give birth in an environment that was calm, quiet, and as natural as possible. My first thought was that the hospital is where the majority of expecting moms have their babies. And that is the place that I had

> **"THE FACT THAT NINETY-EIGHT PERCENT** of babies born at home were able to be breast fed right away is amazing to me and one of the reasons why I chose to delivery at home.**"**

concluded would be my first option. But for some strange reason, giving birth to my baby in a hospital just didn't sit right with me 100%. And because of my uneasiness, I wanted to look into other birthing options.

My searching and enquiring continually led me to hearing about home births and midwifery. Then I researched further into home births, and it led me to a documentary that changed my perspective on the hospital birthing experience. After watching that documentary, I was 100% sure that I was not going to deliver my baby at a hospital. I quickly jettisoned that idea because of what I had learned. Thus, that option was completely out of the question. End of story!

You may be wondering why? Well, all my research consistently led me to the best possible option and course of action for me, and one which had a reliably high rate of success. At the time, my husband was the only person who supported my decision to home birth. Once we resolved in our hearts to home birth, we then set out in earnest to find the right midwife for the task of delivering our baby. In the end, we were rewarded in our efforts because we found the perfect midwife. Unto this day, it remains the best decision I have ever made. I have to admit, however, I was a little sad that the hospital was not going to be the place where I would have my baby. I had always grown up with the belief that hospitals were the only legitimate places for giving birth. But learning more about home births helped me to be confident with the maverick stand I had taken, and I was also really excited to be tackling an issue that is talked about very little in our society.

> **"WITH A HOME BIRTH, YOU WILL RECOVER** much faster, and without the soreness or the grogginess as a result of the medications administered. No surgery recovery needed here!"

HEALTH

If you have had a healthy pregnancy in the past and are a low risk mom, then delivering your baby at home under the watchful eye of a midwife should be a very safe option. Women who have home births tend to experience a much lower rate of interventions such as epidurals and episiotomies during labor. While these interventions may be necessary for the safety and health of the mother and or the baby when complications arise, it is important to point out that women who have planned home births typically give birth to babies that are healthy and safe, without the need for interventions. Additionally, ninety-seven percent of home birth babies are carried to full-term and have an average birth weight of eight pounds. Nearly ninety-eight percent were breastfed immediately and then all the way through to the six-week postpartum visit with the midwife. Significant to note is that only 1% of these babies needed to be transferred to the hospital after birth for further medical care due to complications, and still the majority of these cases were for non-urgent conditions. With my particular midwife, 6% of all her clients on average need to be taken to a nearby hospital because she chooses to take high risk moms under her care. Your midwife is highly trained to determine whether the baby's condition warrants a transfer to a hospital.

> "A HOME BIRTH WILL GIVE YOU THE option of having the most natural birth without all of the typical hospital-associated interventions."

The fact that ninety-eight percent of babies born at home were able to be breast fed right away is amazing to me and one of the reasons why I chose to delivery at home. Granted, I am sure this is possible at the hospital; however, mothers still run the risk of not being able to breast feed their babies immediately for any number of interventions that occur with hospital births. And it is these interventions which pose the greatest threat to both the mother and her baby during child birth because they often lead to unnecessary caesarian deliveries. Which is why more and more moms are opting to deliver at home.

Another very important factor that influenced my decision to home birth was the high rate of cesareans in the U.S. The national average of cesareans performed in the U.S. annually is at an all-time high of 31% for full term pregnancies as compared to the remarkably low rate of 5.2% for other countries, this according to a 2010 "Outcomes of Care for 16,924 Planned Home Births in the United States" research study published in the Journal of Midwifery & Women's Health. When you consider these numbers, it makes me wonder why and how this is possible? Thus, it became obvious to me that if I wanted to eliminate the C-section option from the equation, I would need to pursue the home birth alternative, since it appears now as though doctors are choosing caesarian deliveries over normal births at ever increasing rates. When you consider the well-known health risks and dangers related to cesarean operations and the higher costs associated with the procedure, then that 2010 planned home birth study underscores the benefits of the midwife-led home birth alternative available for expecting

> " A Healthy Breastfeeding mother will help support a healthy newborn's development."

mothers that exists outside of an overburdened healthcare system.

Natural

A home birth will give you the option of having the most natural birth without all of the typical hospital-associated interventions. A big plus is that you will be mentally alert throughout the delivery process because you will not be left groggy or passed out from all of the drugs that they may administer to you at the hospital. This will also ensure that you experience the safest and fastest delivery possible. My home birth experiences lasted three hours on average from the start of the delivery process to when the baby was finally out. I have heard of women being in labor for hour's followed by many of them having to remain in the hospital for several days following certain interventions. With a home birth, you will recover much faster, and without the soreness or the grogginess as a result of the medications administered. No surgery recovery needed here! You will be much more alert and present right after your baby is born. Most moms experience an oxytocin high, which gives them a welcomed boost of energy and excitement to cuddle their babies and start that all-important skin-to-skin contact right away.

You won't have a delay in being able to breastfeed as compared to the breastfeeding difficulties many moms experience behind C-sections. This is mostly because of certain hospital protocols that get in the way of the natural order of things. When a new mom undergoes a C-section, she will typically also experience a delay in the onset of milk production due to the disruption of the hormonal cascade pathways that lead to the production of her baby's nutrient-rich breast milk. Mothers who choose the natural, home birth option don't experience this problem. To be more specific, prolactin is the hormone that is released by the anterior pituitary gland that stimulates a mother's milk to start flowing after childbirth, and it is known as the "mothering" hormone. It increases during pregnancy and peaks when labor starts on its own. Continued prolactin production during and after labor prepares a woman's body for breastfeeding. Prolactin, it is widely believed, may also play a big role in moving labor along and helping the newborn adjust to life outside of the womb. It also aides in jumpstarting a woman's caretaking instincts and helping her to adjust to being a mother. A healthy breastfeeding mother will help support a healthy newborn's development.

> **" WITH A HOME BIRTH, MOST WOMEN** enjoy a strong feeling of empowerment throughout the entire pregnancy and child delivery process.. **"**

Another important hormone is Oxytocin, commonly known as the "love" hormone. This important hormone is release by the pituitary gland, and it plays a key role in our ability to bond socially. It is also crucial to sexual reproduction. And it is on the scene during pregnancy, increasing more significantly during active labor and

Why Home Birth?

childbirth. Both the mom and baby produce oxytocin after birth. And as long as your baby breastfeeds, he or she will continue to produce this hormone. It's presence during labor is vitally important because it plays an important role in causing increased contraction of the uterus during labor.

Having a natural birth comes with many benefits. You have to carefully evaluate the pros and cons of giving birth to your baby via the home birth option, so that you can rest assured in the end knowing you made the best decision possible. Ultimately, you must really want this for you and for your baby. With a home birth, most women enjoy a strong feeling of empowerment throughout the entire pregnancy and child delivery process. And afterwards, they feel such an overwhelming sense of accomplishment for defying conventional norms to bring their babies into the world the all-natural way. Despite having to endure the pain, many women will gladly choose this birth plan for each subsequent pregnancy they have. As far as I'm concerned, it was the best decision I have ever made. My home births have all been very safe, fast, and rewarding. I chose to home birth for many reasons; however, the driving force behind my decision was that I wanted give birth as naturally as possible so that I could give

> **" THINK ABOUT IT...FOUR HOME BIRTHS,** no complications, no meds, no C-sections, and no impersonal hospital environments to make me feel like a bit role player in one of the most important events a woman can ever take center stage for.**"**

my children the best odds at the healthy start possible coming into this world so that they could pursue their God-given destinies once they arrived.

NEWS FLASH! Before I could complete this particular chapter, I gave birth to my fourth child via home birth. I'm delighted to say that my baby is healthy and that the delivery went very smoothly. Think about it…four home births, no complications, no meds, no C-sections, and no impersonal hospital environments to make me feel like a bit role player in one of the most important events a woman can ever take center stage for. Why not be the lead in your next production by having a home birth?

Chapter Two
FINDING THE RIGHT MIDWIFE

Midwifery has existed for millennia in societies all around the world — long before hospitals appeared on the scene to supplant the role that midwives have played in bringing life into the world. You can even find mention of the role of the midwife in the first chapter of the book of Exodus in the Old Testament of the Bible. In verses 15 through 21 of that chapter, we read how Pharaoh commanded two Hebrew midwives to destroy every male baby that they delivered, while permitting the females babies to be born. In the end, they disobeyed the king's cruel edict and were rewarded by God for doing so. I highlight that Biblical story simply to illustrate how far back this noble profession extends, and yet, that story still does not go back far enough to show us just how long midwives have been around.

In this particular chapter, I would simply like to help you to find the right midwife to suit your situation. Keep in mind that the average midwife will bring just as much experience and knowledge to bear on your pregnancy as an ob-gyn. The big difference will become quite evident in terms of the very reasonable cost of her midwifery skills versus the price tag that accompanies your doctor's degrees and credentials. But for most women, this difference pales in comparison to the difference in the quality of care you will enjoy with a midwife as compared to an ob-gyn. I would first like to take a look at the general role you can expect a midwife to play in your pregnancy.

> **" Keep in mind that the average** midwife will bring just as much experience and knowledge to bear on your pregnancy as an ob-gyn.**"**

Role of a Midwife

Midwives are highly trained health professionals who assist healthy women in the delivery of their babies during natural childbirth. They are on hand to help expecting moms during every phase of pregnancy, remaining by the mother's side throughout the nine months of pregnancy, during delivery, and well into her postpartum recovery. Midwives are trained and equipped to deliver babies at their client's home, at a birthing center, or even in a hospital setting. Her main mission is to ensure the safe and natural delivery of your baby. Midwives are trained to educate, advise and provide comfort and support to birthing women. They are constantly on the lookout for potential and actual complications. If necessary, they are prepared to provide emergency treatment until the attention of a medical team can be obtained.

In every state of our union, midwives are regulated and licensed by a midwives board to ensure their competency to practice midwifery and to ensure their ongoing training and development. In some states like Texas, the midwifery board defines midwives as the practice of providing the necessary supervision, care and advice to a woman during normal pregnancy, labor and the postpartum period. They are to provide natural birth of a child and to provide ongoing care for the newborn all the way through to the sixth week after delivery.

Midwives offer holistic care that encompasses the needs of the well woman, including the specific needs of the adolescent, pregnant, postpartum, peri- and post-menopausal woman. More specifically, their care includes antepartum, intrapartum and postpartum care for the mother and pediatric care for the newborn. Midwives view pregnancy and birth as normal, natural and healthy events. In fact, a woman can turn to her midwife for just about all of her health needs, including annual exams, prescriptions, and contraceptive counseling. They also discuss your particular blood type to factor in any potential complications that may arise while you are under their care. For example, if you are

> **" MIDWIVES VIEW PREGNANCY AND** birth as normal, natural and healthy events.**"**

RH- and need prenatal or postpartum RhoGAM, your midwife will discuss your particular treatment options. If your blood type is negative, then she can test your baby's blood type at birth to determine whether or not you will need postpartum RhoGAM to prevent Rh sensitization that can lead to hemolytic disease with your newborn.

Care Provided

Midwives support and assist you physically and emotionally during the labor and birth of your baby. They use no pain medication during childbirth, employing only natural birthing methods to assist you in having a heathy and gratifying birth experience. Immediate postpartum care will depend on your unique circumstances and needs. Some states require their midwives to apply infant eye prophylaxis within two hours after giving birth. Therefore, depending on the requirements of the state in which you live, your midwife may be required to apply eye drops or ointment to your baby's eyes to protect him or her against any unknown infections you may have. Your midwife will encourage you to breastfeed your baby immediately upon delivery. This was something that I was all too excited to do with each of my newborns. I wanted to nurse them as soon as they were born.

> " It is not uncommon for midwives to address your issues in a manner that impacts your physical health as well as your emotional and psychosocial well-being."

Finding the Right Midwife

Midwives take a great deal of pride in the fact that they are very hands-on with their patients. And because of the special bond that forms between them and their patients, it is a well-known fact that these health professionals provide a level of care and support that goes way beyond the traditional doctor/patient relationship. It is not uncommon for midwives to address your issues in a manner that impacts your physical health as well as your emotional and psychosocial well-being. A good midwife is truly worth her weight in gold because she can be to you a well of knowledge and wisdom on a vast array of issues that impact women, from relationship issues to sexual problems.

> **" Before the labor and delivery** phase, she provided me with a list of items that I needed to obtain for the home birth — which needed to be purchased before the 37-week appointment."

But I would like to give you an idea of some of the services you can expect to receive from your midwife — but from my personal experiences. Please keep in mind that my midwife was by my side for the birth of all four of my children. My midwife's services included the workup of my complete medical history, an initial physical examination, a test to screen for gestational diabetes and anemia, and routine, current health assessments. This also gave her the opportunity to monitor my pregnancy on a constant basis to stay on top of any problems that might surface. She was on call for me and my baby 24 hours a day, seven days a week. She provided a full range of services, beginning with early prenatal care, which allows for early detection of potential and actual complications with either the mother or the baby. She constantly emphasized wellness and always encouraged healthy living through a nutritious diet and moderate exercise. She was quick to let me know that she couldn't guarantee that my baby would be born at home because in cases of emergency, there could arise a need to transfer care to a hospital either during delivery or postpartum. She did recommend that I have my baby examined by a pediatrician in the first 36-42 hours after the birth — which was something that I had to set up prior to delivery.

My midwife reassured me constantly throughout the process that I could request a transfer of care for me or my baby at any point. If there was an emergency during my labor or immediate postpartum, she assured me that she would call 911 and that they would make the appropriate transfer of care. Some midwives may have you do two written birth plans — one for the home birth and the other in the unlikely event of a transfer of care — keeping all involved parties clear as to YOUR desires. At the end of the day, the only thing that really matters to your midwife is the health of you and your baby.

Before the labor and delivery phase, she provided me with a list of items that I needed to obtain for the home birth — which needed to be purchased before the 37-week appointment. She indicated that she would provide the specialty equipment. She also provided me with a worksheet of information at my 37-week appointment so that I could apply for the birth certificate and social security card. She did ask that they be completed before the baby was born.

After deliver of my baby, she provided me with about five postpartum visits. At these visits, she checked the health of my baby and me, and she spoke with me to find out how the baby and I were doing. These visits started 36 hours after the baby was born and continued weekly thereafter. She provided me with copies of the newborn exam to provide to my pediatrician. These visits included the footprints of my baby — which I always requested extras for my keepsake album and for the birth certificate. Also during these visits, she would weigh the baby and perform exams to see if the baby needed any medical assessments. I really enjoyed these appointments. They were precious moments during which I kept my camera at the ready. And because each of my babies grew so accustomed to hearing my midwife's voice while in the womb, they were always so responsive to her voice during these visits.

> **" When I left the facility that day, I knew that Mary was who I wanted as my midwife."**

The Interview

When I first interviewed my midwife (we'll simply call her by her first name, which is Mary), I really didn't know what to say or the questions I should ask. She gave me her background and told me how many successful home births she had performed, which I found to be impressive. At the time, I had no idea just how popular home births were. My main concern, however, focused on everything from what would be discussed in the appointments to what would take place during the actual delivery. This was my first baby, so I had no clue as to what to expect. At the time, Mary was the director of a local home birthing center in my home town. She gave me a tour of the facility, which was set up for water births. Each room had a birthing tub and the supplies needed for a baby's delivery. From everything I was taking in, I gathered that most home births are water births. This particular facility gave expecting moms the option to have a water birth or a bed delivery. Seeing the entire operation for the first time gave me a sense of relief. Prior to this visit, I was totally unaware that alternatives existed outside of traditional hospital settings where women could give birth to their babies. Observing the professional staff members doing their jobs and seeing the birthing tubs and other supplies gave me a great sense of comfort, especially since it presented me with more options for delivering my baby.

> **" It is also imperative that you get** along well with her because, after all, the two of you will spend a great deal of time together during nine months of pregnancy and roughly six weeks thereafter."

One thing I noticed right away was how calm and pleasant Mary was. She struck me initially as a person who was very warm and caring. I felt at ease with her immediately, which allowed us to carry on conversations that seemed to continue endlessly. Her explanations regarding the whole natural birth process were very clear and easy to understand. In fact, Mary took the time to fill in the blanks on issues with my first pregnancy where my doctor felt it not necessary to explain certain things to me. I found this to be very reassuring. I quickly warmed to her candidness, which was strange because we had just met. When I left the facility that day, I knew that Mary was who I wanted as my midwife. My husband and I both agreed that we didn't need to interview anyone else and that she would be the one to guide us through the home birth process.

You have to be very comfortable with the midwife you choose. It is also imperative that you get along well with her because, after all, the two of you will spend a great deal of time together during nine months of pregnancy and roughly six weeks thereafter. Getting the selection right the first time has led to my husband and me having the same midwife by our side for all four of our home births. And because I wanted no one else but her, we have spent the last ten years getting to know one another very well. Therefore, do your homework and choose wisely.

> " **WITH MOST DOCTORS, YOU END UP** waiting longer in the waiting room than you do actually in their presence."

OB-GYN VS MIDWIFE

What To Expect From Your Home Birthing Experience

With my first home birth experience, I found myself in the weird predicament of seeing a midwife and an ob-gyn at the same time. Being completely unaware of the natural birth option at the beginning of my first pregnancy, I began the process by seeing an ob-gyn. Shortly thereafter, I learned about home births. I would look forward to my appointments with my midwife, but I also had to continue to keep my appointments with my ob-gyn doctor. Needless to say, I was in a very sticky situation. The time I spent with Mary during appointments was significantly longer than the brief sessions I spent with my doctor, and Mary was much more generous with the information she shared about my situation, as well. Without exaggerating, we would spend on average about three hours at each appointment.

> " After you have enjoyed the privilege of having all of your prenatal appointments in the comfort of your home, you will be loath to want things any other way."

Her prenatal care included a complete medical history, a physical examination, a test to screen for gestational diabetes and anemia, and a health assessment at each session. This also gave her the opportunity to monitor maternal weight gain, blood pressure and uterine growth. She kept a record of all the information. She made sure I took my vitamins and that I kept plenty of liquids in my body. She also made sure I was doing well emotionally, since a woman's emotional wellbeing can affect the pregnancy. She also did a urinalysis for the early detection of any potential complications, such as anemia, toxemia and diabetes. At every appointment, she would also determine the fetal position of the baby. We would hear the baby's heartbeat with Doppler ultrasound technology. I found it very enjoyable to be able to hear my baby's heartbeat from the comfort of my own bed. One of the things I found fascinating at these appointments was how Mary could, with a simple touch, determine the exact location and position of my baby. Nowadays, doctors must rely on sophisticated gadgets to do what came naturally to my midwife. She would tell me, "Oh! Here is a leg, or there's her foot". Then I would feel with my own hands to confirm the accuracy of her skills. I thought it was amazing how she knew exactly where the baby was by relying on mere touch. I found these moments the most enjoyable and memorable of all. Being able to know that you have a baby growing inside and being able to pinpoint where all the movements were coming from left me awe-struck.

> **" THIS INDICATED TO ME THAT MY MIDWIFE** was right on track with my ob-gyn, even though my doctor had to rely on high tech equipment to achieve the same results."

If there were certain issues with my health or physical well-being, Mary made sure to address them immediately. She stayed on top of my moods and how I was feeling throughout my pregnancy. Mary was on call for me 24/7. If there was something that I was confused about or a feeling I had on a particular issue, she was always there to address my concerns.

What To Expect From Your Home Birthing Experience

What I valued most about Mary was that she valued my time just as much as I did hers. When we scheduled appointments, she always arrived promptly. No waiting forever like in a doctor's office, only to been seen by him or her for only a few minutes whenever they do walk into the room. With most doctors, you end up waiting longer in the waiting room than you do actually in their presence. If there where records from another health care provider, she would request to see them, and we would review them together. She would explain the contents of my records in laymen's terms so that I could understand what was going on. No talking down to me or leaving anything out for fear that I couldn't understand. If I wanted a sonogram, I would arrange that with her, and she would recommend the various locations around town where I could obtain one.

> " I WAS SO PROUD OF MYSELF FOR sticking to my guns and going through with having a home birth. But boy did she scold me something fierce."

After you have enjoyed the privilege of having all of your prenatal appointments in the comfort of your home, you will be loath to want things any other way. Yet, I still had appointments to keep with my ob-gyn. This strange predicament I found myself in gave me a very unique perspective, and I was able to realize a lot of things. First of all, my ob-gyn appointments were very long, but only in the waiting room. At times, I was greeted by unfriendly staff who would tell me to be seated and that they will be right with me, only to be called an hour later — well past the scheduled appointment time. Whenever I finally did get into one of the rooms to see the doctor, I was again met with endless waiting before she would arrive. By the time the doctor eventually came in, I would be so tired and worn from waiting that I would usually forget all the questions I wanted to ask her.

They would perform the usual check of my vital signs and make sure there was no sign of anemia or any other pregnancy-related problems. It would literally take about 30 minutes in the room for the doctor's assistants to perform these checks, and then finally the doctor would come in for the last 10 minutes, only to discuss the test results and when I needed to schedule my next appointment. That would be the extent of it — short and to the point. It seemed as though the doctor gathered just enough information to satisfy the minimal requirements for that session before moving on to the next appointment.

At the end of my appointments with my midwife and those sessions with my ob-gyn, I began to notice that the results of my time with each of them produced the same information. This indicated to me that my midwife was right on track with my ob-gyn, even though my doctor had to rely on high tech equipment to achieve the same results. I found it strange that my midwife would use her hands to arrive at the same conclusions my doctors reached by utilizing state-of-the-art equipment to determine the positioning of my baby inside the womb.

What To Expect From Your Home Birthing Experience

With my first pregnancy, I had a female doctor who was very friendly at first but who was also very set in her ways. She figured it was either her way or no way, at all. When I mentioned to her that I wished to have a home birth, she pretty much flipped out. She made me feel as though it would be impossible to give birth without the aid of a doctor, and she even questioned why I wanted to go this route, to begin with. I was not armed at the time with much of a defense to buttress my position on the issue. Neither did I possess much knowledge back then to counter the wave of condescension coming from her direction. I couldn't explain with much evidence why I wanted a home birth. I only knew deep down that I did. I only shared with her my wishes on this matter in hopes of getting a small measure of support from her. But more importantly, I also wanted to see if she would be there for me and my baby in case an emergency arose during the home birth. She flat out told me NO that she wouldn't and that it was a crazy thing for me to do. In the end, I kept her as my doctor because I was too far along into my pregnancy to switch to another doctor.

> " **If you don't currently have a doctor** who can agree with you on the home birth issue or can at least simply respect your decision on the matter, then find one who will. "

So, at all of my appointments with her, I simply towed the line and told her only what she wanted to hear. Her appointments were very short and basic. There was no sense of caring or concern that I could detect from her during any of my appointments. I still, however, ended up paying her standard doctor's fee as though she would be the one to deliver my baby, in addition to the hospital fee. This was, after all, my plan B in the event that something did go wrong with the home birth. In that unlikelihood, I knew that I would at least have a room ready for me at the hospital, should I need it.

Then she did not hear from me for several weeks. My due date passed, and I still had not notified my doctor or the hospital that I had already given birth to my first baby from the comforts of home. After experiencing my first successful home birth, I did end up seeing her a few weeks afterward. To say that she was shocked to see me is an understatement. I stopped by her office so she could see my baby girl. I was so proud of myself for sticking to my guns and going through with having a home birth. But boy did she scold me something fierce. She was so upset at me for having done what I did. She questioned my rationale and stated, "This was not supposed to be like this". She wouldn't even look at my baby or even congratulate me for doing it on my own without the aid of any type of pain medications. I was in complete shock. As a woman and mother herself, I thought she'd be a bit more understanding. For her not to see that this was something special for me was a bit disheartening, especially because a home birth is a huge accomplishment that very few

> **" NEEDLESS TO SAY, MY MIDWIFE** outshined both doctors I encountered regarding my pregnancies.**"**

women get to experience. I was so hurt and disappointed by her response. From that moment until this day, I have never again gone back to see her.

If you don't currently have a doctor who can agree with you on the home birth issue or can at least simply respect your decision on the matter, then find one who will. In my case, I had come into the knowledge of home birthing a bit later than I would have liked with my first pregnancy. As a result, I was forced to proceed with a doctor who was adamantly opposed to my views on the topic of natural birth. But with my second baby, I was determined to find the right doctor who would either share my views on home birth or at least be sympathetic to them.

> " **BUT WHO CAN BLAME DOCTORS?** They are simply defending a system that feeds and supports them. "

With my second baby, I did find a doctor who agreed with me, however slightly, on this issue, and he agreed to be there for me in case of an emergency. I found it very ironic that the doctor who would eventually support my decision to home birth would happen to be someone of the opposite sex. Go figure! In fact, he further believes that a woman should not be induced unless there exists an actual emergency. To me, that positon alone spoke volumes about his overall approach to the practice of medicine. When I told him about my first home birth, he simply remained quiet and seemed a little surprised at how well it had gone. I mentioned to him that I would do it all over again, and again he remained quiet. He did, however, indicate that he preferred that I have my next baby in a hospital setting, and he promised to have on hand all the necessary accommodations for me to deliver my baby as naturally as possible.

Fearing that if I appeared too unyielding that I might evoke similar antagonistic feelings with this doctor as I had with the former one, I presented to him the impression that I would keep an open mind on the matter. This approach served my needs very well. As has proven to be typical with most doctors, his appointments were also very brief, and they too lacked the necessary detail to fill in the gaps. Needless to say, my midwife outshined both doctors I encountered regarding my pregnancies. When I did go to my appointments with him, I would always question him about the safety and possibility of having my second baby at home. He would try to create doubt by pointing out that although 99 percent of the time things will be fine, you still must be concerned about the one percent chance that something could go wrong. That told me everything I needed to know — that yes, I would be just fine having my baby at home.

> "THE CARE I RECEIVED FROM MY MIDWIFE was just so much faster, healthier and more effective in terms of getting rid of my symptoms."

At every appointment, he would encourage me to have the delivery in the hospital, but I would remain quiet, knowing that I planned to continue with my birth plan and have my baby at home. Not once did he try to discourage me from having the baby at home by belittling my decision, as my previous doctor had. However, he did make it abundantly clear that he preferred that I be in the hospital when my due date arrived. But who can blame doctors? They are simply defending a system that feeds and supports them. It's what they work for, and it's what they know best. They have too much at stake to endorse other child birth options.

SICKNESS DURING PREGNANCY

While I was pregnant with my second baby, I experienced a lot of sickness because my pregnancy happened to be during the fall and winter months when I was most prone to the cold and flu season. My midwife was always available to help me get over my colds. She would recommend certain medicines and herbs to take that would be safe for me and my baby. When I did call my doctor for the first time to ask what would be safe for me to take, getting an answer proved to be a long and arduous process. I would have to send in my doctor's notes or prescriptions if it was in fact a cold that I had contracted. By the time I would finally get my answer, it was just too late to make any difference, at all. And in many cases, the process just proved to be too much work. It was never just a quick call. I would always have to leave messages with the assistant, and by the time doctor would return my call, typically several days later, I was feeling horrible because my condition had gotten much worse. So, I just stuck to calling my midwife because the process was significantly faster, simpler, and safer. For one thing, I knew she would recommend something that was all-natural, which was a huge plus for me.

> **"THERE IS SO MUCH MORE SUPPORT** and one-on-one care with a midwife. They are literally only a phone call away."

Second, I knew that her recommendations would work. She always followed up on how I was feeling the next day. The care I received from my midwife was just so much faster, healthier and more effective in terms of getting rid of my symptoms.

So, this goes to show that you can expect to experience a big difference in both the quality and level of responsive care you will receive from your midwife versus the kind of service you are bound to get from a traditional ob-gyn. There is so much more support and one-on-one care with a midwife. They are literally only a phone call away. For those who need that kind of support and care, this is truly the way to go. With a midwife at your side, you will have a safe and healthy pregnancy because she will literally be there every step of the way — there to hold your hands through the morning sickness as well as through the complications brought on by any unexpected sickness.

Therefore, when trying to find the right midwife, make sure you do your research so that you will be able to interview each candidate fully armed with all the necessary questions that will help you to sift through the pile of hay to find your needle. Who knows, maybe you'll be fortunate to snag your catch the first time out, like I did. Here's to your success!

Chapter Three
MY FIRST HOME BIRTH

As I had indicated in chapter one, I always imagined that I would give birth to my children in a hospital. In fact, I had no idea it could be done any other way. The thought of delivering a baby at home never enter my mind...until certain concerns continued to nag at me. I figured that the well-being of my baby depended on the choices I made and that it was up to me to get it right the first time. As a result of this mental inquisition taking place within, I set out to find answers.

And my research consistently pointed me in the direction of home births. This natural method of bringing babies into the world seemed to address every concern I had about how to safely deliver my baby without all of the attendant drugs that are involved with the traditional methods. But as good as home births are, I would like to be up front and completely honest with you about my first home birth experience. While it had a happy ending, the opening scene of the postpartum delivery was a bit sketchy, to say the least.

But the one piece of advice I would like you to take away from this particular chapter is that the role players in your home birth process are indispensable assets. Not only is your midwife crucial to the successful delivery of your baby, but also a highly trained doula is a must have member on your team because she and your midwife will work in tandem to get you through some tough times in your pregnancy.

The Services of a Doula

With my first pregnancy, my husband and I took a few birthing classes that were administered by a doula. A doula is a trained, non-medical birth coach who is there with you before, during, and after the natural birth process. She does everything possible for you to go through the labor pains without the need for an epidural. A doula is there to provide the mother with emotional, physical and informational support, but in no way is she there to replace a medical doctor or a midwife. Her services are there only to comfort and help you to relax and feel less stress while giving birth.

My doula gave me a lot of guidance and support. The classes where once a month, and they would cover many topics related to child birth. She explained in great detail how a natural birth typically plays out, the various ways to lessen the severity of labor pains, and what to expect when you are in active labor. She also discussed the things a mother should look out for when her baby arrives. The classes were very helpful and gave us a good indication of how the overall process would flow. I would definitely recommend that you attend these classes if they are available to you. Whether offered by a doula or a midwife, the benefit to you would be priceless.

> "A DOULA IS A TRAINED, NON-MEDICAL birth coach who is there with you before, during, and after the natural birth process. She does everything possible for you to go through the labor pains without the need for an epidural."

Going through the classes and having an idea of what to expect taught my husband and me to track and time my contractions. A month before my due date, the midwife brought all the items she needed for the birth. She prepositioned the items at my home so that all she had to do when the time came was to simply jump in her car and rush to the scene. Her preparation package included things like an oxygen tank, medicine, gloves and a host of other items for the birth. She also gave me a list of items that I needed to have on hand in the birthing room for when the baby arrived.

False Labor

It was two weeks prior to my due date when I first experienced some rather untimely contractions. At first, they came light, but gradually they started to increase in both intensity and regularity as time went by. Given that this was our first baby, we notified the midwife of the timing of the contractions and the pain that I was feeling. Responsive to my condition as always, my midwife and doula were at my home within 30 minutes. My midwife explained how the breathing should go, and she helped me get through each contraction. It was about 9 p.m. by this time, and they were

> "**My midwife ended up waiting all** night in my home to see if maybe they would start up again, but they never returned. I felt horrible for wasting her time."

there by my side, providing emotional and physical comfort. Then all of a sudden, the contractions stopped. They simply ceased, and I was just there waiting for the next one to begin. But nothing happened. She then massaged my feet to see if they would start up again. But nothing!

My midwife ended up waiting all night in my home to see if maybe they would start up again, but they never returned. I felt horrible for wasting her time. But she assured me that this was normal. She indicated that the baby was just not ready to come and that I had simply experienced a false labor. This incident, I believe, was just preparing me for the real thing. So, she went home, and I resumed my normal routine.

Then about a week and half later, I began experiencing the labor pains again. By this time, however, I had a pretty good idea of what to expect. My husband got the room ready by dimming lights. We even lit a candle and put on some relaxing spa music to lighten the mood. We knew we wanted this

My First Home Birth

experience to be as calm and silent as possible. Prior to our false labor scare, we had read that delivery can be a traumatic experience for both the mother and her baby. Therefore, we sought to have a silent birth. More on that in the next chapter. We mentioned our desire to the midwife, and she agreed that our special moment should be as calm and quiet as we could possibly make it.

REAL LABOR

When a hint of the real deal began knocking, I waited till the contractions were a little closer together. I was able to walk throughout the house to get through that initial wave. Since they weren't coming as often as expected, I distracted myself by looking at photo albums, and I even told my husband I wanted to take a nap. This was around 10 p.m. when the pains began their ebb and flow rhythm. So, I took a nap while my husband stayed up watching over me to make sure I was able to doze off to sleep. It was around 3 a.m. when I woke with very strong contractions. By this time, my midwife and doula had already arrived. My husband had called them both while I slept through the pains. The nagging pains continued to mount their aggressive assault against my body, but we were dutiful to write down the time between each contraction. I walked around, trying to get

> **"I STILL HAD MY BABY ON MY CHEST** when all of a sudden I felt as though I was going to faint. I alerted the doula as to my condition, and she was there to get the baby before I blacked out."

through each episode while the doula massaged my lower back and applied ice packs to relieve some of the pain. Meanwhile, the midwife prepared the tub with warm water to have ready for when I needed to begin delivery.

While in the bath tub, I was actually able to relax a bit more. The warm water was soothing, and I was able to catch my breath. Then the contractions started again! The midwife explained how they would proceed from here on out. She instructed me on how to breathe. While in the tube, she checked the baby's heartbeat several times to see if it was normal. She then asked me if I felt the need to push — which I did. By this, I had been in the tub for roughly 45 minutes when, all of a sudden, I felt the urge to push. She then explained to me how I should push during my contractions. She made sure I would stop pushing when I needed to stop. We maintained strong communication throughout the ordeal. She was always very sure of exactly when and for how long I should push.

> **"I WAS OUT FOR A FEW MINUTES.** I didn't come around until the midwife jolted me back to consciousness by putting a strong smelling substance under my nose."

In the middle of one of my pushing moments, my water sake spilled out in the tub, which was a normal occurrence, and it alerted me that my baby was on the way. I must have pushed a few more times just to help my baby to make her way into the world, while my husband was at the other end ready to catch her the moment she appeared. Her head come out first, and she was under the water for a few seconds before completely emerging after what seemed an eternity. After they pulled her out of the water, my baby took her first breath. As soon as my husband secured her in his arms, he gently placed her on my chest. They then put a warm blanket over her, and the midwife was able to clean her while she lie there on my chest. She suctioned her mouth and did a quick once over to make sure she was okay. Thank God, she was.

My Health Scare

While she was on my chest, the midwife warned me that I would feel small contractions and that I needed to push out the placenta. And sure enough, within minutes it was out. At that point, she examined it to ensure that it had completely been excreted. I still had my baby on my chest when all of a sudden I felt as though I was going to faint. I alerted the doula as to my condition, and she was there to get the baby before I blacked out. I was out for a few minutes. I didn't come around until the midwife jolted me back to consciousness by putting a strong smelling substance under my nose. She tried putting an IV on my hand, but my veins just disappeared; therefore, she was unsuccessful going this route. She also noticed that the tub of water began turning a strong red color due to my profuse bleeding. At that

> **"With the Pitocin swiftly administered, the bleeding soon stopped, but not before I had lost nearly a pint of blood."**

moment, she determined that I needed Pitocin.

Pitocin is a natural hormone that causes the uterus to contract in order to induce labor, but it also causes the uterus to contract after delivery to prevent postpartum hemorrhaging. In my case, I needed my uterus to return to normal since my body was not doing it on its own.

With the Pitocin swiftly administered, the bleeding soon stopped, but not before I had lost nearly a pint of blood. With so much blood loss, I was too weak to get out of the tub under my own strength, and thus, I had to be assisted.

After a few minutes in the tub, I was able to get out and lay on the bathroom floor, while oxygen was being fed into my system. While all this was happening, the doula had my baby in her arms. Wrapped in a blanket, she began to fuss because she was getting pretty hungry. Meanwhile, the oxygen was helping me to recover strength, and they gave me lots of Gatorade and various other sugary drinks to get my blood sugar levels back to normal. With strength to get in bed, they placed my daughter on my chest where I was able to nurse her right away. My midwife gave me a quick lesson on how to ensure the baby was properly latched onto the nipple. Before you know it, we were both in tune, and she was able nurse.

> "**THE FIRST PERSON I CALLED WAS** my mom. Since she was totally unaware of my home birth plan, she was in total shock when she got the news."

The whole process took about three hours from the point of my strong contractions to when she was fully delivered. After having her, I was able to eat right away. My baby never left my sight. While I rested in bed, the midwife and my husband cleaned up the room, and we were able to notify family and friends that I had given birth. The first person I called was my mom. Since she was totally unaware of my home birth plan, she was in total shock when she got the news. I never told her about how my first birth went because I knew I wanted more children, and I also knew that I also wanted them delivered in the same way. As result, I did not want to have to deal with my mom's concerns and objections.

> **"Although I was not mentally** prepared for what had occurred with my first home birth, my midwife, on the other hand, knew exactly what to do to respond to the situation and stabilize my situation."

Admittedly, my first home birth was a very scary experience; even though, what I went through is rare for healthy, first-time moms. Prior to finding out about natural, home births, I would never have chosen to go through something like this. The midwife told me after all was said and done that I must have lost about a pint of blood. She further told me that if I delivered at the hospital, I most likely would have needed a blood transfusion. Given that I was at home, I simply needed to eat iron-rich foods and lay in bed for a couple of days. There are a few reasons to explain why my situation played out the way it did. For one thing, I come from a family of bleeders. This condition is part of my family history. The second reason is that during my pregnancy, I was taking iodine. At the time, I was seeing a holistic doctor who told me that iodine is very good for brain development in babies. Therefore, I added that vitamin to my prenatal regimen every morning. My midwife attributed my excessive postpartum bleeding to the iodine in my system at the time of my delivery.

Although I was not mentally prepared for what had occurred with my first home birth, my midwife, on the other hand, knew exactly what to do to respond to the situation and stabilize my situation. She had all the necessary medications and tools available so that she was able to deal with my situation in a timely matter. After I had recounted the entire chain of events to my sister, she revealed to me that the same thing happened to her when she gave birth to her baby. They only difference was that she was at a hospital. She also mentioned that her uterus was not able to contract after her delivery and that the hospital staff had to give her Pitocin, as well. My aunt had a similar experience in the hospital, and they had to do a blood transfusion due to the large amount of her blood loss. I never would have had these conversations with my family members if I had not gone through my own harrowing child

> "Though not something we like to talk about, women need to discuss their delivery experiences with close family members, if for no other reason than to help someone prevent experiencing a similar event, if possible."

birth experience.

Though not something we like to talk about, women need to discuss their delivery experiences with close family members, if for no other reason than to help someone prevent experiencing a similar event, if possible. Sharing with my midwife the conversations I had with my sister and aunt, she indicated that had we known about my family medical history, there was a strong chance that my situation could have been prevented, or at least better precautions put in place to anticipate and mitigate its affects.

> "Given that this was my first planned home birth, I was very careful to tell only certain individuals because I didn't want people to judge me or questions my actions."

Unknown To Parents

Given that this was my first planned home birth, I was very careful to tell only certain individuals because I didn't want people to judge me or question my actions. If I mentioned my decision to someone and they reacted negatively, I would kindly tell the individual to refrain from expressing their opinions and to say nothing further to me about the matter. Handling others' views in this way helped me to block out any negative influences and unwelcome remarks that I didn't need to hear, which could cause me to second guess my decision.

To be very certain, my mom was completely against the

home birth idea. So, I was especially careful not to mention anything to her. My mom wanted to be very involved with my pregnancy, and I sincerely appreciated that. I know that most mothers dream about being there for their daughters through every phase of the pregnancy. But when my mom expressed staunch disapproval of home births, I accepted her position and spoke no more to her about the matter. With my first birth, I kept the arrangements I had made with the hospital in place just in case I needed a backup plan. I even went so far as to tell my mom that the hospital was where I had planned to deliver my baby. She, however, was completely unaware that I had my plan A arrangements already made with my midwife. Throughout my entire pregnancy, my mother never met my midwife. To this day, I feel bad for deceiving my mom in this way, but I only wanted to assure her that everything would be fine.

> "I firmly believe that if you have at least one person who supports your decision and will be by your side at your home birth, then that is all the support you need."

Prior to my home births, my mom had no knowledge of the concept. And because she had experienced three successful hospital births, I can fully appreciate her misgivings with delivering babies any other way. I firmly believe that if you have at least one person who supports your decision and will be by your side at your home birth, then that is all the support you need. In my case, my husband was my solid rock. He agreed with me, and he was going to be there with me while I delivered my baby. His support was all that mattered.

Once I had my baby at home, however, my mom was the first person we notified. I simply told her that I didn't make it to the hospital and that the urgency of the situation necessitated my delivering at home. Of course she was shocked! Once the news sunk in and she saw me — healthy and in stable condition, and after holding her perfectly healthy granddaughter in her arms — that's when I told her everything that had transpired to bring our baby girl into the world. At that point, she neither argued with me nor every again raised any objections to the idea of having a home birth.

What I did with my first child behind her back has now occurred three subsequent times in the light of her approving eye. And because of the four beautiful grandchildren I blessed her with, my mother is able to bear witness daily to how successful home births are.

Chapter Four
THE SILENT BIRTH SECRET

A fter successfully going through my first home birth, I had to take a moment to reflect on how everything had transpired. I also needed to discuss with my husband and my midwife the things that went as we had planned as well as those things that went wrong. More importantly, though, we needed to take a closer look at the things that could've gone even worse than they had. At the end of the day, however, I delivered a healthy baby girl, and I quickly returned to a healthy condition within a few hours after giving birth. My husband and I both agreed that the midwife and doula we chose for our home birth team were the perfect fit for our situation. By my side, they ensured that things went well.

In all honesty, however, I had to take a moment to question whether having that home birth was the right decision, or not. Would the delivery have gone differently in a hospital setting as opposed to how events played out in my home? Once again, my husband and I agreed that it probably wouldn't have been any different in a hospital. We felt that Mary handled the delivery very well. Looking back at my first home birth, I still feel strongly that I made the right decision. And in that moment of reflection, I concluded that I would do it all over again. One important factor that played a big role in the success of that first delivery was our decision to have a "silent birth".

> "One important factor that played a big role in the success of that first delivery was our decision to have a "silent birth"."

You may be wondering what a silent birth is and why it is so named? Another name for this type of delivery is a quiet birth. All it means is that your entire delivery takes place in a calm and quiet setting, whether at home or in a hospital environment. It also means that no one is permitted to talk or make any inappropriate comments during the birthing process, so as to decrease the likelihood of trauma the baby may experience as it is being separated from the mother during delivery. I feel that in the delivery room no one should be instructing and yelling at you to push or trying to rush you along the delivery process.

I first learned about the silent birth concept while I was, at that time, reading about the latest trends in child delivery. And when I stumbled upon the term silent birth, I thought to

The Silent Birth Secret

myself, "What's that?" So, I did a little research, and I discovered that Dianetics pioneer L. Ron Hubbard is the creator of the silent birth procedure. He believed that birthing women should be calm and in a quiet environment while giving birth. Hubbard further felt that the room should be in complete silence and that the mother should be the only person permitted to say anything during delivery in order to prevent the mother and baby from experiencing any stress beyond that produced during normal child birth.

So, when I mentioned to my midwife that I wanted to experience a silent birth, she agreed without any hesitation; even though, she had never heard of the concept prior to me discussing it with her. During my first birth, we all remained very calm and quiet while going through the delivery process. When she had to speak and instruct me at various points during delivery, she would simply whisper her instructions in my ear. On the other hand, the doula and my husband stood by quietly awaiting any instructions the midwife needed to give them. If they had to speak, they also kept their words to a whisper. To this day, what stands out the most about my first home birth is the peace and calm that pervaded the delivery room. To further improve the atmosphere, we dimmed the room lights so that it wasn't too bright. As a result of the softer lighting, I noticed that my baby was able to open her eyes immediately upon delivery. Under

> **"Every birth should be a** peaceful time, and you should be in a very serene environment."

the bright hospital lights that typically welcome babies, they are not able to open their eyes until they are moved to a room where the lights are much softer on the eyes. So, when my baby was born, she entered a very tranquil environment where everything was as peaceful as we could make it.

Because labor alone is a very intense moment, you will want to create a peaceful and stress-free environment — an atmosphere where nobody is yelling or screaming, or where weird comments aren't being belted out, such as "push" or "hurry up". In an environment with so much shouting, your baby is going to be welcomed into a stressful situation. With a silent birth, there are no doctors or nurses in your face barking out commands like a drill sergeant, causing your stress levels to escalate tremendously. Every birth should be a peaceful time, and you should be in a very serene environment. I believe that delivery is a time when the mother needs to concentrate on what she is doing. Her mindset needs to be clear and uncluttered because birthing a child requires tremendous mental strength and endurance.

> **"I TRULY BELIEVE THAT 60% OF THE** delivery ordeal is mental. I kept telling myself that it was incumbent upon me to deliver my baby the best way possible, and for me, it was via the silent birth method."

You must realize that pain and discomfort accompany the delivery of any baby, but those unwelcome feelings will quickly subside the moment you hold your baby in your arms.

Therefore, having a clear and focused mindset during delivery will more likely than not lead to a peaceful end result. People often ask me how was it possible for me to go through a home birth without any medications to ease the pain. I truly believe that 60% of the delivery ordeal is mental. I kept telling myself that it was incumbent upon me to deliver my baby the best way possible, and for me, it was via the silent birth method.

Benefits

The great health that all my children enjoy is something that I am very proud to witness daily. My kids are very easygoing children who don't stress out easily. In public, they are very relaxed and low maintenance. They are never hyperactive, nor are they the types to run around uncontrollably. I'm not sure whether to attribute their pleasant dispositions to the very low sugar diet they've all been on since birth or to the silent births that welcomed each of them into the world, or to the delayed cord clamping (more on this in chapter six). However, I'm certain that my children are the beneficiaries of the positive effects of all three, since they are all blessed to have the same good-natured dispositions.

People constantly ask me what I do to my children to get them to be so calm and peaceful all the time. Even around other rambunctious children, mine remain very pleasant to be around. Don't misunderstand me! In no way am I implying that if you have a silent birth that your children won't be hyper-active or prone to mischief. What I would like for you to get from this chapter, however, is that a silent birth will result in a calm and peaceful delivery. The silent birth method is a very healthy and wise procedure to practice in any home birth or hospital delivery room. Having done four silent births, I can't imagine bringing a baby into the world in the midst of screaming and bright lights.

> **"Having delivered all four of my** children, Mary now incorporates the silent birth approach into all of her deliveries."

Having delivered all four of my children, Mary now incorporates the silent birth approach into all of her deliveries. She has adopted this practice because it creates a calm setting in the room. She even told me of a time when she almost kicked a father out of the birthing room because he was being too loud. This is serious business. When she calls for quiet in the room, that is what is expected. For her to have adopted the silent birth concept simply validated my decision, and it means that I discovered something truly remarkable and worth emulating.

Environment

Well, you may be wondering just how a silent birth should be carried out. It's a very simple concept. There should be absolutely no taking in the birthing room. The lights should be either turned off or dimmed. My midwife got around the room by using a small flash light. For two of my births, we did have relaxing music playing very softly in the background. For a moment during those two births, I felt like I was in a spa. We even had candles turned on in the room. Once we all agreed to be quiet, everyone spoke only in a whisper from that point on.

If you can't have silence in the room, then at least your midwife should demand that those individuals allowed to be in the room refrain from making any loud coaching instructions or disruptive comments. What you are simply trying to avoid is having the baby hear any startling noises that can trigger stress. Again, I would like to emphasize that the mother is the only person in the room who is permitted speak above a whisper or be loud. After all, she is the only one going through the stress and strain of child birth. If she feels the need to yell or scream, that is her prerogative.

For some strange reason, I wanted to remain absolutely quiet when I went through each of my silent births. In explaining the methodology of silent births, Mr. Hubbard emphasized that the mother should be the only one permitted to say anything she needed to communicate in the birthing room. However, I believed differently about the matter. I felt that I needed to be totally quiet, and I even felt that I should not scream or make any loud noises. But in

> **"THE LIGHTS SHOULD BE EITHER** turned off or dimmed. My midwife got around the room by using a small flash light."

all actuality, it is completely up to the mother as to the volume level of communication she wishes to permit in her delivery room. All in all, I found my silent births to be remarkable experiences.

In closing...

Having a silent birth is, in my opinion, the least stressful and most peaceful way to deliver your baby. I have been blessed to experience four successful home births. They have given me a rare perspective on how babies should arrive in this world. For that precious moment to be filled with silence and peace makes your experience so much more memorable and rewarding. I see it as the first priceless gift that I gave to my children — a gift that carries with it lifelong benefits. As a result of my personal experiences with silent births and because of the benefits I have witnessed with my four children, I am a staunch advocate of this birthing concept. And should I decide to have more children, I would employ the silent birth method with those births, as well.

Chapter Five
MY SECOND HOME BIRTH

After having a scare with my first homebirth, you would think that I wouldn't want to venture down that road again. Well, I'm here to tell you that I did it again. And although successful, the second homebirth was completely different. Granted, there was a lot to reconsider behind my first homebirth scare, but in the end, the baby was healthy, and I recovered rather quickly. And now, I am even more aware of what can go wrong. I stayed in touch with my midwife after the birth of my first child, and I was delighted to have her by my side to help me with my second baby. By the time my second pregnancy rolled around, she had grown to know my entire family very well. She was well acquainted with our home environment, and she was more than familiar with how the first birth played out, so much so that she prepared this time for every conceivable scenario.

But my concerns with this pregnancy were vastly different

from the first one. For starters, the size of my second baby was significantly larger than the first child I delivered. Second, I experienced great concern when my delivery date was projected to go past my expected due date. And third, with my second pregnancy, I had a doctor with this pregnancy who somewhat agreed with my

> **"With this second attempt, I quickly learned that every pregnancy is different and every birth presents its own challenges."**

birth plan. Once again, and it bears pointing out, I learned something very important about the natural birth process that should never be downplayed, and that is the importance of having a water birth. With this second attempt, I quickly learned that every pregnancy is different and every birth presents its own challenges.

I hope that after reading this chapter you would still choose to deliver your baby naturally via homebirth and that you would exit on the other side of your delivery with your own success story.

Different Doctor

My second pregnancy was very different from the first one. To begin with, I had a completely different doctor who mildly supported my decision to have a homebirth. I wanted to continue seeing an ob-gyn in addition to my midwife. He was much more understanding of what I wanted for my birth plan. He was more open to the idea of me delivering at home.

He refrained from weighing-in with his opinion on the matter. He refused to comment either way. After experiencing the mistreatment I had with my first ob-gyn, you're probably wondering, "Why again?" I wanted to continue with any ob-gyn more out of the comfort and peace of mind it gave me than anything else. I wanted to ensure that I had a viable plan B in place just in case anything went wrong with my plan A. In a worst case scenario, I would need to be transferred to a hospital, and I wanted the comfort of knowing that the hospital contingency had been factored into my planning. So to reiterate, continuing to see an ob-gyn was more of a comfort for me.

My appointments with him were short and sweet; everything was straight and to the point. Yet, as with my first ob-gyn, his medical assessments were the same as my midwife's. Given that he was a male doctor, I was surprised to discover that his chairside manner was much more pleasant than that of the female ob-gyn I had with my first pregnancy. However, he did try to convince me at every appointment to have the baby in a hospital setting. To sweeten his position, he promised that he would not induce labor or have any other interventions, unless necessary. He also stated that he would not have anyone interrupt me during my delivery. But his promises did little to change my mind because I knew that

> "**But his promises did little to** change my mind because I knew that when you are in a hospital, you are on their turf and must ultimately play by their rules."

when you are in a hospital, you are on their turf and must ultimately play by their rules. Thus all promises, as well-intentioned as they may

> **"THE SIZE OF THE BABY REMAINED** a source of concern throughout the pregnancy. I began to wonder myself if I could still deliver this baby at home."

have been, would be out the window if the hospital deemed them to be a conflicting nuisance. And what if he were to be out of town when I went into labor? I would then be left alone to try and convince the attending medical staff of my doctor's promises to me, and I was not going to take a chance on that. As with my first baby, I was determined to have a silent homebirth.

Furthermore, there would be no way for me to control the lighting in a hospital room, and I'm certain they would not have obliged me on this small issue. And for me to demand that everyone coming in and out of my delivery room remain silent would have been totally out of the question. Just the thought of me having a silent birth anywhere other than my home seemed an impossibility. So, whenever my doctor raised the issue of me having a hospital birth, I just gave him a smile and said, "I will think about it." But all the while, I maintained my plans to have a homebirth, as I had with my first pregnancy. This time around, however, I felt more prepared for the establishment opposition I would face. I did do one thing differently, though, and that was to change my vitamin regimen this time around. I made it a point take less iodine to avoid a repeat of what happened with my first delivery.

My Second Home Birth

Size and Timing

Another concern I had was the size of the baby that was growing inside me. At every appointment, my doctor told me that my baby was measuring at a weight he should have weighed two weeks prior. The size of the baby remained a source of concern throughout the pregnancy. I began to wonder myself if I could still deliver this baby at home. With my small frame, my doctor recommended that I not attempt to push out such a big baby. Nowadays, C-section is the "a la carte" menu item when a woman faces the delivery of an oversized baby. The thought of that was freighting to me. One of the main reasons I first looked at homebirths to begin with was to avoid having a C-section delivery. Hospital C-sections are at an all-time high, and they will use any excuse to schedule you for this risky procedure. I knew that in order for me to avoid this type of delivery altogether, I had to have my baby at home, or there would be no other way around this battle.

> "Although he never voiced his displeasure with my decision to have a homebirth, he did warn me that mine might be a difficult delivery due to the size of the baby. But in the face of his fears, I turned to my midwife for her reassurances."

Both my doctor and midwife predicted that I would have a baby that weighed anywhere between eight to nine pounds. My midwife looked at my weight gain, and with the use of her hands to feel how the baby was positioned, she knew that he was going to be big. My doctor was the one who was worried. Although he never voiced his displeasure with my decision to have a homebirth, he did warn me that mine might be a difficult delivery due to the size of the baby. But in the face of his fears, I turned to my midwife for her reassurances. I simply asked her whether she felt that it was okay for me to proceed with our birth plan, given the size of the baby. I felt reassured when she told me that everything would be fine. I gained significantly more weight with my second pregnancy than I did with my first one. Being pregnant in the winter months did not help at all with my weight, since you find any excuse to eat more! Despite my midwife's reassurances, I continued to be a bit concerned about all the weight I had gained, nevertheless. I had a lot of lower back pain due to the weight that I was carrying. But with every concern or pain I had, she was there to guide me through them.

> "**THE DAYS AND WEEKS WENT BY,** and my due date was getting closer, and still my baby exhibited no signs that he was ready to face the world."

My Due Date

Of great concern to me with my second pregnancy was the fact that I went over my 39 weeks. The days and weeks went by, and my due date was getting closer, and still my baby exhibited no signs that he was ready to face the world. I was pregnant during the holidays, and my midwife and my doctor both predicted that this baby would arrive before Christmas. Their prognostication had me on edge because doctors tend to take their vacations during this time of year. I wasn't worried about my midwife not being there because once she had me on her schedule to deliver my baby, she made it her priority to be there for me during this important time. Please keep in mind that if your delivery date coincides with a holiday, please make sure that the person delivering your baby will not be taking vacation during the time you need him or her the most, whether that individual be your doctor or your midwife. As we all know, the holidays are a time for family, and there is a higher than normal probability that your provider will not be available as promised. So, do your research so that you'll not be left all alone.

> "**One thing I did not want** to get fooled by was false labor like I had been with my first pregnancy."

Because I chose to have a homebirth without any interventions, I had to simply wait until he was ready to come out. By this time, I was getting very anxious because I was at my 39th week, and he still was not ready to come out. At this point, I just wanted to get this baby out. However, like my midwife, my doctor does not like to induce labor unless it is absolutely necessary; although, he did indicate that he would need to intervene if I went beyond the 41st or 42nd weeks. On the other hand, my midwife told me something completely different. She indicated that when the baby is ready, he will come out in his own time — which meant either two weeks before or two weeks after the due date. She was not at all worried that I was going passed my expected due date. I took solace in the fact that she was not worried!

My due date was getting closer, and still I exhibited no signs of needing to deliver. Keep in mind that once you are given a due date, you can, in all actuality, deliver either two weeks before or two weeks after that date. But since my baby did not come two weeks sooner than expected, it now meant that he could safely go two week past my due date. To top it all off, they keep telling me that my baby was measuring two weeks bigger than normal, and I even thought that I was going to deliver two weeks early. Boy, was I wrong! I did not give birth until my actual due date at 40 weeks.

I remember that morning waking up and wondering why was I still pregnant! I just couldn't believe that I had reached my due date and that I was so huge. I tried to just go about my day and remain as calm as possible. I had read that a woman could stimulate contractions by walking around. So, that's one thing I set about to do plenty of. That morning, I went for a long walk to try and get my mind off the fact that I was still pregnant. I had my two-year-old daughter with me, which helped to keep me going.

We took a long walk, and it was about late afternoon when I had my first bout of labor pains. I thought, "Okay, we'll start to pay close attention to them from here on out." So, I started writing down the time that they started as well as their duration and intensity. One thing I did not want to get fooled by was false labor like I had been with my first pregnancy. I really wanted to make sure this was the real deal. I meticulously tracked the time of the pains, and believe me when I say they were actual labor pains. As I continued, I told my husband, "We need to go because I think this is it. I need to go home." We were close by, and we made it home without any issues. My mom was there because I had asked her to pick up my daughter so that my husband and I could run some errands. She did not know that I had planned another homebirth. I told her that I had decided to deliver at the hospital. I did not tell my mom that I was going to have a homebirth because I still didn't want to hear any negativity regarding the issue; even though, she did not have much to say anymore on the topic. Still, I chose to also keep my second homebirth a secret from her simply to avoid hearing anything unwelcoming.

> "WITH A WATER BIRTH, YOU ARE able to calm down and relax more because the buoyancy of the water relieves a great deal of the stressful body weight off of your frame."

Meanwhile at home, the pains got stronger and stronger, and they were more painful than ever. But still, I had to get my mom out of the house because I did not want them present during the delivery. This was a very stressful and difficult time for me because I was lying to my mother — a woman who had proven to be nothing but supportive of me all my life. Nevertheless, we made up a story about where we were going, and we asked her to watch our daughter for a while. By this time, it was tuff lying to my mom because she just kept looking at me and commenting how much my stomach had dropped. Repeatedly, she kept telling me, "Look at your stomach. You're going to deliver." She was pointing out the obvious, which was that my stomach had dropped significantly.

By now, the pains were intensely painful. Every time I felt the onset of contractions, I would simply go into another room so my mom could not see my agony and so that I could simply ride out the storm. When I would return after the contractions had passed, I would try very hard to put on my game face, hoping she was none the wiser. So, when the moment seemed right, I told her that we had to leave, and I asked her to take our daughter. I indicated that I would be back to pick her up in a little bit after running our errands. Eventually, she finally left and took our daughter with her. As soon as the front door closed behind her, I hurried upstairs and got dressed and ready to deliver my baby. I told my husband to call Mary because the pains were getting more intense. A little while later, she showed up ready to get down to business, as everything she needed was already prepositioned in the room and prepared in advance.

> "**WHILE I WAS GETTING READY TO** push, I felt an overwhelming need to stand up. I felt that I needed the assistance of gravity to help me get this baby out."

Once they got the tub prepared with warm water, that's when I was finally able to get in and take a load off. The warm

My Second Home Birth

water relaxed me, and I was able to recharge and get some energy. I was also able to drink some much needed liquids. While in the tub, I kept adjusting to find a comfortable position, as this was a big baby I was about to deliver. Because of his size, I needed help in any way that I could get it. In the tub, I was able to move around and eventually find a comfortable position to deliver. While I was getting ready to push, I felt an overwhelming need to stand up. I felt that I needed the assistance of gravity to help me get this baby out.

> **"As with the first delivery,** Mary also kept the umbilical cord attached to my son until the blood-rich nutrients stopped pulsing through it."

Once I was able to stand, my husband and midwife were there every step of the way to assist me as I needed them. I followed Mary's instructions on when to push because I wanted to avoid damaging myself while pushing out a rather large baby. After only a few pushes, my son popped out and he looked prefect. And voilà, I just experienced another successful homebirth.

Once my son was out and in my arms, I realized in that moment that I had done it again. I had just gone through the most painful experience in my life. Although it was a calm, silent birth, I have to admit that it was truly painful and exhausting, albeit well worth it. While holding my son, Mary was able to examine him and make sure he was healthy. She cleaned him off, and we stayed in the tub a few minutes longer. Once my placenta was out, Mary was ready with the Pitocin

> "**With my first pregnancy, I** never questioned whether to have a bed delivery or a water birth. To be quite frank, I really didn't put much thought into which method I preferred."

injection, which she administered immediately to avoid a repeat of what happened with my first delivery. As with the first delivery, Mary also kept the umbilical cord attached to my son until the blood-rich nutrients stopped pulsing through it. Therefore, she delayed having my husband clamp the cord until the last possible moment. I was more aware of the many delivery-related tasks Mary performed this time around versus the first time I delivered.

So, while I held my baby in my arms, I noticed a container nearby where she placed the placenta. Minutes after my baby was delivered, he was still attached to the umbilical cord to take in max residual nutrients from the placenta. I was able to get out of the tub, walk over to my bed, lay down, and begin nursing my son. While in my arms, he looked content and peaceful. Indeed, he was a well-developed, nine pound baby boy.

Doctor's House Call

At Mary's suggestion, I needed to identify a pediatrician prior to the birth of our baby who would be willing to make a house call in order to examine our newborn. We were very fortunate to have a family friend who was also a pediatrician and who was willing to assume that responsibility. Since my son was born on a Sunday, we waited to call him the next day. He was rather pleased to hear that I had delivered at home and that everything had gone well. That afternoon, he made it to our home carrying his black medical bag. He performed a thorough examination and confirmed to us that the baby was well and in good health. Needless to say, this was great news to us!

If I was not able to have a pediatrician come to the house, then I would have had to make an appointment and take the baby to his clinic. However, we were grateful that he was willing to make a special house call on our behalf. If your midwife recommends that you select a pediatrician to be on hand to serve as that second set of eyes, make sure you do your research so that you will find one who will accommodate your home birth situation. Also, you will want to find a doctor with whom you feel comfortable working. This was, after all, his second time coming to our home after the birth of one of our children. He made a house call behind the birth of our first baby, and his latest visit was to make sure everything was okay with our second child. I was pleased with his bedside manner, and he never questioned my decision to have a home birth. He simply noted the good health of my babies and left soon after his business was finished. However, he did suggest that I make follow up appointments so he could see them in his office and start the wellness checkups there. Which after a

> **"I TRULY RECOMMEND HAVING A WATER** birth whether you are having a small or large baby. Being able to have a calm, less stressful, more mobile, and speedy labor is reason enough to go this route."

few weeks, I did end up taking the baby to his clinic.

If it is not possible in your case to get a doctor to make a house call, then there is nothing wrong with you taking the baby to your doctor's clinic. But again, we were fortunate to have a family friend who also doubled as our pediatrician and who was willing to do house visits after the births of our two children.

WATER BIRTH

With this second delivery, I was able to walk much sooner than with my first delivery; even though, I experienced more pain the second time around. One key thing I learned from my second birth is the importance and many advantages of having a water birth. I feel that it was the most important factor that contributed to me being able to deliver a nine pound baby, especially with my petite body structure. With a water birth, you are able to calm down and relax more because the buoyancy of the water relieves a great deal of the stressful body weight off of your frame. It also takes the labor pains away and helps you regain a great deal of energy after going through the stress of the contractions.

> "I WAS ABLE TO DEFY CONVENTIONAL thinking and prove that even a petite woman who is pregnant with a nine pound baby can give birth safely from the comforts of home."

I feel that my contractions were less intense once I got into the water. After all, delivering in water helped me deliver a nine pound baby at home, without pain medication. Why? Because a water birth will calm you and help you move more effortlessly through the delivery process. When you get into a warm water, you can move about more freely and find the comfortable positions you would like to be in while delivering. I am a very petite person, and for me to be able to deliver a nine pound baby at home without pain medication is not very common nowadays in a hospital setting without the mother having to endure a dreaded C-section. I definitely would have had to undergo a C-section or have interventions if I had delivered my son in a hospital.

Although my first child was delivered via water birth, I did not realize the immense benefit of giving birth in water until the birth of my second child. Because my first baby was of a normal size, my mobility was not hindered during delivery as much as it was with my second child. And boy did the water play a crucial role in easing a great deal of discomfort during my second delivery.

With my first pregnancy, I never questioned whether to have a bed delivery or a water birth. To be quite frank, I really didn't put much thought into which method I preferred. My midwife simply assumed that I would be giving birth at home and that I would do it in a warm tub. From her professional standpoint, that made the most sense in terms of a woman's comfort and ease of delivery. But after the tremendous ordeal of delivering a nine pound baby, I never questioned by which method I would deliver my last two children. Water birth became my only option because of my second delivery.

Being in a warm water tub while giving birth to a rather large baby aided me tremendously. It helped me to have a speedy labor and also to go through labor without needing any anesthesia. When interviewing to hire a midwife, make sure that water births are in her repertoire of delivery methods. Although my midwife allows each mother to choose her own delivery option, she is not shy in making it know that water births are her preferred method.

When she first come to our home, she did ask to see the tub and the area where I would deliver the baby. She approved of the location and thought the tub's size was appropriate, as well. If, for some reason, you do not have access to a tub or the tub space is not big enough to accommodate a water birth, your midwife should be able to suggest other delivery alternatives. For example, if you don't have a tub in your home, then there are inflatable water tubs available for labor purposes only.

I truly recommend having a water birth whether you are having a small or large baby. Being able to have a calm, less stressful, more mobile, and speedy labor is reason enough to go this route.

Chapter Six
UMBILICAL CORD

My second home birth went smoothly, and it felt easier simply because I knew what to expect. For the second time, I had a happy baby and a peaceful delivery. But boy was this one painful due to its size. Yet again, I was able to deliver my baby without the need for pain medication. I had to give myself a pat on the back because this was one tough delivery, but I succeeded for the second time at natural birth. And I attribute a great deal of success to positive thinking and mental preparation. Having gone through another successful birth, I had to take another moment to think things through. I was amazed to have had two successful home births, given that they were both very different in many ways, and yet, they were similar in the procedures that took place immediately after the babies were delivered.

I had so many questions after this second birth. For one

thing, I wanted to how it was possible that I, being so petite, could have such a big baby? I also wanted to know how it was possible that I could have gone into labor on my actual due date? Why did we wait to clamp the umbilical cord when it stopped pulsing? So many questions raced through my mind. And as quickly as they came, so too would come their answers. With the delivery of my second baby, I now had two births against which I could now make comparisons. I was able to analyze and ponder the pros and cons of two successful home births.

> "**Why does my midwife have** her delivered babies remain attached to the umbilical cords for as long as 15 to 20 minutes after the baby is born?"

What became apparent to me rather quickly after the birth of my second baby is how vital the umbilical cord is to the life of babies and how they should remain attached to it along as possible after they are delivered. As far as home births go, knowing the proper time to clamp the umbilical cord is something that I needed to know more about. Why does my midwife have her delivered babies remain attached to the umbilical cords for as long as 15 to 20 minutes after the baby is born? Why doesn't she choose to store the umbilical cord blood cells in an umbilical cord bank like the healthcare industry strongly encourages nowadays? I had to get the right answers for these questions that were running through my mind.

Placenta Awareness

As soon as I delivered my second baby and held him in my arms, nothing else seemed to matter. The importance of how the placenta and umbilical cord work to provide life-sustaining nutrients to my baby during the pregnancy and for several minutes postpartum was the last thing on my mind after I had just given birth. In fact, with my first birth, I didn't even know that I was caring around the placenta for several minutes after I had delivered my baby. After my second birth, however, I was fully aware that my baby was still attached to the umbilical cord, but I had no idea that it was even possible until I took notice of it for the first time. I'm the type of person who can't stand to see excessive bleeding or broken bones. That's the reason I wanted nothing to do with viewing it when I delivered my first child. I was a little scared to see something that I was not going to be able to deal with later.

But I can tell you that my fears were baseless because when I took a quick glance at that placenta for the first time, I didn't experience any nauseating reaction. It simply lay there, very still and nonmenacing. There was nothing to be frightened about. It simply looked like a piece of meat you might find in a grocery store. Well, that's the closest thing I have to compare it. With my second birth, I was able to muster a bit more confidence to take a closer look at it. I had to remind myself that this organ came from me. So, although the placenta might be something you are presently afraid to look

> "**IN FACT, WHEN IT COMES** supporting the life of your baby in utero, the placenta is worth every bit of its weight in gold."

at like I was with my first delivery, I would recommend, however, that you take a close look at it and familiarize yourself with how it looks because there is nothing to be grossed out about. In fact, when it comes supporting the life of your baby in utero, the placenta is worth every bit of its weight in gold.

Now in a typical hospital delivery setting, as soon as the baby is born, the placenta is quickly discarded and the umbilical cord is immediately cut. However, such a procedure leaves the extra blood just sitting there in that severed cord. Mary, on the other hand, did not cut the cord right away. She let the cord stop pulsing before she clamped it. She waited about 15 to 20 minutes before completely cutting it. She also did a thorough examination of the placenta to ensure that it was fully intact and that none of it was left behind. I remember holding my baby in my arms with the placenta still attached. They simply placed it in a covered container, and I barely even knew it was there. Because that extra blood was still flowing and pulsing through the umbilical cord, my midwife kept it attached until the blood ceased to flow through to my baby.

Before the baby and the placenta are delivered, the unborn infant depends on its mother for oxygen and nutrients. During pregnancy, the placenta forms and attaches to the uterus whereupon the unborn baby gets its life-giving blood and nutrients from the placenta via the umbilical cord. Therefore, during the nine months in the womb, the baby subsists on a portion of the mother's blood that flows through the placenta. And because unborn babies get all their oxygen from the placenta-provided blood, they do not begin utilizing their own lungs until they are born. For this reason, my midwife kept the umbilical cord connected until all of the oxygen-rich blood ceased flowing through it. The vital lesson to take away is that your midwife should allow the umbilical to remain in place until all of the blood from the placenta ceases to pulse through to the newborn. Therefore, until the blood stops flowing, the umbilical cord should not be viewed as waste to be discarded as soon as the baby is delivered.

> **"Therefore, until the blood** stops flowing, the umbilical cord should not be viewed as waste to be discarded as soon as the baby is delivered."

When my midwife would check the baby's heart rate, she would allow me to hear the swooshing sound of the placenta, which results from the mother's pulse delivering blood to the placenta. But it never dawned on me that this temporary organ was responsible for providing my baby with nutrients, waste removal, heat regulation, and gas exchange through the mother's blood supply.

So, after birthing the placenta, I saw that it was still attached to my baby. While holding him in my arms, I thought to myself, "Oh, OK! There it is; that's what it is." It never occurred to me just how important the placenta is to the life of a baby or just how nutrient-rich it is. With my first and second births, Mary did not clamp either cord right away. But I still had not given much consideration as to why. Because I had my husband there with me and because I trusted him completely, I simply relied on him to clamp the cord. What happened to that cord or the placenta was not my concern as long as I was able to hold my baby soon after the delivery. That's all that mattered to me at the time.

I do remember, however, with my first delivery, my doula asking me what I wanted to do with the placenta. I thought, "I don't know what to do with that blob of flesh. What is it for and why would I want to keep it?" She did mention to me that the placenta is full of nutrients and that it's a very good source of nutrition. She asked me if she could have it. To which I said, "Of course. I don't know how to dispose of it or even know what to do with it." So, she asked for my permission to keep it, and I agreed that she should take it. She said she was going to plant it near a tree in her yard because it would provide the tree a rich source of nutrients that you can't find anywhere else. Again, I did not put much attention on the matter. I simply figured that with her knowledge as a doula, she would know best what to do with the placenta.

> **"She said she was going to plant** it near a tree in her yard because it would provide the tree a rich source of nutrients that you can't find anywhere else."

By the time my second delivery rolled around, I was fully aware of the post-delivery ritual. My baby would be delivered followed by the placenta; the umbilical cord would be clamped; and the placenta would be allowed to remain by my side so that my son would continue to receive its nutrients—even if only for a few more minutes. However, this time, my midwife expressed interest in my placenta. Mary straight out asked me what I planned to do with the placenta. As with the doula, I told her that I didn't want it and that she could have it. I went on to tell her that I had no need for it and that I wouldn't even know what to do with it, to begin with. So, Mary took it.

> "Later, I asked Mary what she did with my placenta and all the others that she has collected from her patients. I was surprised to learn that she uses them for various things."

I realize now that there is plenty of research and different programs that advocate freezing the umbilical cord for future benefit, such as for saving lives because cord blood is rich in stem cells, which is useful in the treatment of various diseases. In my case, I chose to allow my daughter and my son to benefit from that iron-rich blood rather than turn it over to a hospital to be frozen. Both my daughter and son got an extra boost of nutrients that continues to fuel their good health to this day. Thus, one benefit of the delayed cord clamping includes an increased volume of blood transfer from the placenta to the child by as much as a third after it is outside the womb. Additionally, delaying the clamping also allows for an increase in an infant's storage of iron. Finally, both of my children received a higher count of red blood cells, stem cells and immune cells, as well. The extra iron they received is very beneficial for brain development.

My daughter and my son have been very healthy all of their lives, and neither of them has ever been sick to the point where they needed to be hospitalized. My daughter and my son have caught the common cold over the years, but I can honestly say that in all their respective eight and six years on this planet, I can count on one hand the number of times they have had to visit the doctor. I attribute this to the delayed cord clamping.

Later, I asked Mary what she did with my placenta and all the others that she has collected from her patients. I was surprised to learn that she uses them for various things. She uses them to conduct further research with her students. Because placenta contains small veins that run throughout the organ, she also teaches them the skill of phlebotomy by drawing blood from it. Additionally, she uses them to teach her students how to perform sutures by having them remove pieces from the placenta and then having them sew the flesh back together. So, instead of burning them like hospitals do, she uses the placentas for further research. As you can see, Mary is able to extend the placenta's benefits far beyond what babies enjoy while in the womb. Yet, most pregnant women aren't even aware of the many blessings their placentas provide.

> "However, what was different is that I now had a student asking me what I planned to do with my placenta."

Having experienced two natural births and discovering how amazing placenta is at nourishing babies inside the womb and for several minutes postpartum, I can now fully appreciate the life-sustaining properties the placenta possesses and why my midwife and doula desire them as much as they do. In an upcoming chapter, you will discover why I finally decided to keep the placenta from my third birth. And at that delivery, I had another person (Amber who was a student going through the midwifery program) shadowing Mary and assisting her throughout the duration of my third home birth.

The third time around was no different than the first two deliveries. I delivered the placenta; they checked to ensure that it was intact; and once again, they delayed clamping the cord. Then Mary waited until it stopped pulsing before finally cutting the cord. However, what was different is that I now had a student asking me what I planned to do with my placenta.

> "**Placenta encapsulation is the** practice of ingesting the placenta after it has been steamed, dehydrated, ground, and put into a pill or tablet form."

While I was recovering, Amber approached and asked me what I intended to do with the placenta. I told her that I wasn't sure, but I asked her what she did with them. That's when she said to me, "Let me take it, and I will encapsulate it for you to take in order to recover faster. Amber took my placenta home with her, and she somehow turned it into pills for me to take. The process is called Placenta encapsulation.

Placenta Encapsulation

Placenta encapsulation is the practice of ingesting the placenta after it has been steamed, dehydrated, ground, and put into a pill or tablet form. The mother then takes the pill to benefit from the numerous health benefits that it provides.

When I received the encapsulated pills from my placenta, I started taking them right away. I would take one every morning, and I felt great for the rest of the day. I felt energized, and I just felt good about myself. My bleeding was gone by the second week, and I produced milk for the baby in abundance. I had zero problems nursing. The pills lasted me about 2 months. The amount of pills you get really depends on the size of the placenta that you have. The pills were about the same size of small gel-like capsules. They are not too big, but neither are they too small in size, either. The pills were not difficult to swallow, and they did not have an aftertaste.

> "I wish I had known about them with my first two pregnancies; however, I was delighted I had the opportunity to benefit from them with my third delivery."

I can definitely say that compared to my first two deliveries, I recovered much quicker after the delivery of my third baby. And I attribute the faster recovery to the placenta pills I took. I felt more energized. Keep in mind that I had two other children to look after in addition to my newest addition. Therefore, I needed all the energy I could get. I never experienced any bouts of postpartum depression after the birth of my third child, and neither did I suffer from any hormonal imbalances, either. I simply felt really good about myself and I was genuinely happy to see my family after the grueling ordeal of delivering a baby. Taking the placenta tablets caused me to recover much faster and they helped me to produce significantly more milk than with my first two pregnancies.

> **"As you look for a midwife,** identify someone who practices delayed cord clamping and who knows how to encapsulate your placenta."

Some of the known benefits of taking the placenta pills include a speedier recovery after delivery, increased milk production, hormonal stabilization, replenishment of depleted iron levels, and a speedier return of the uterus to its pre pregnancy state. I can personally attest to experiencing all of the stated benefits of taking the placenta pills. They are truly remarkable. I wish I had known about them with my first two pregnancies; however, I was delighted I had the opportunity to benefit from them with my third delivery.

In closing…

I hope that you will take advantage of the information I shared in this particular chapter. From the delayed cord clamping to the Placenta encapsulation, these two nuggets alone will lead to greater health benefits for you and your baby. As you look for a midwife, identify someone who practices delayed cord clamping and who knows how to encapsulate your placenta. My babies continue to benefit to this day from the delayed cord clamping performed on them as newborns. They received a higher numbers of red bloods cells, stem cells and immune cells during the delayed cord clamping while blood was still flowing from the placenta through the umbilical cord to the baby. This is benefit enough to require that the attending midwife perform the procedure after you deliver your baby. Delayed clamping provides essential life support for the baby, and it also protects them from organ and brain injury. The encapsulating of the placenta is a remarkable thing that women need to take advantage of. Who knew that this organ was so valuable long after the delivery process was complete…that it could be used as a nutrient supplement for moms recovering from childbirth. You and your baby will enjoy an overall better postpartum experience by following the advice I outline in this chapter.

Chapter Seven
MY THIRD BIRTH

By now I thought I was a pro at this home birth thing, having two successful ones under my belt at this point. After the birth of my second baby, I stayed in touch with my midwife, Mary, because I wanted to keep her close should I need her services again. You would think by my third birth things would be even easier since I knew exactly what to do. I didn't have any concerns about the delivery aspect of the pregnancy, but somehow I knew that things were going to be different. Overall, I was confident that this third time around I was going to have a quick delivery. Although it turned out to be successful, some things about this one were very different. This goes to prove that every pregnancy is different and every birth is different. Whether you are in the same home setting with the same midwife, things can still go in an entirely different direction very quickly.

HEALTHIER APPROACH

With this pregnancy, I wanted to try something that I had not done with the first two. Since I was pregnant during the summer, I stayed active throughout the duration of my pregnancy. I continued to exercise and play tennis. Being a recreational tennis player, I continued to play the sport while my stomach grew larger with each passing month. I knew that I would have a healthier pregnancy if I stayed active. I had heard that women recover faster and experience speedier deliveries when they remain active during the pregnancy. I delivered my first two babies rather quickly with a start-to-finish average of about three hours. Nevertheless, I wanted to find out whether I could decrease the delivery time even further by maintaining a healthy exercise regime throughout my pregnancy.

> "**Despite my growing belly, an** hour on the tennis court twice a week was sufficient time for me to get the exercise I needed to stay in healthy pregnancy condition."

It's important to note that I also kept the same ob-gyn doctor (from my second pregnancy) who had acquiesced of my home birth wishes. He was in full agreement that I should continue playing tennis until I felt the need to stop. At the time, I thought this approach was wise, given that I wanted to enjoy a faster recovery as well as lose the pregnancy weight faster. With that in mind, I continued playing tennis till I was about eight and a half months pregnant. Let me tell you, it was great! I felt very fit, and my energy levels were very high as a result. Despite my growing belly, an hour on the tennis court

My Third Birth

twice a week was sufficient time for me to get the exercise I needed to stay in healthy pregnancy condition.

I strongly recommend that you stay as active as your midwife or doctor allows, especially if your pregnancy is in synch with the summer or warmer time of year. By following a healthy workout plan throughout my third pregnancy, I did recover quicker, and I did lose my pregnancy pounds much sooner than I had with my first two pregnancies.

Birthing at Home with Existing Children to Care For

With my third home birth, I should point out that I already had two little ones at home who also needed my attention. My focus was constantly divided by two, and it didn't matter to my first and second born children that I was now getting ready to deliver their sibling. Having a homebirth while you have kids in the house is still doable. However, you must put in place a very good birth plan that details what you are going to do when your due date arrives. Your plan must address who's going to look after your children when you go into labor.

> **"Your plan must address** who's going to look after your children when you go into labor."

In my case, I had indicated to my midwife beforehand, as part of my birth plan, that I didn't want to have my kids in the room with me when I gave birth. That's one conversation you must have early on with your midwife so that she knows what your plans are. In the beginning, my husband and I created a plan that listed who would look after them. When and where I would go into labor remained a nagging thought throughout my pregnancy because I wanted to plan for every possible contingency. With my first pregnancy, I went into labor in the early morning hours, but I did not have any other kids at home to be concerned about. By the time my second pregnancy rolled around by late afternoon, I had in place a solid plan that outlined where my daughter would go for a few hours. With my third pregnancy, I had no idea whether I was going to deliver in the early morning or late afternoon. Because an exact delivery time is such a big unknown, you must, therefore, plan for the uncertainty by developing a simple yet comprehensive birth plan together with your midwife and then make it know to everyone.

> **"I thought the third birth** was going to be a piece of cake; therefore, I decided to wing it and just have the baby on the bed."

A Non-Water Birth Experience

The change of scenery with my third birth created a bit of confusion, and it also threw off a routine that I had grown to expect. For starters, I was not in my own home by the time I delivered my third baby. We were renting a home because my husband and I were in the process of having a new home built. Having a water birth was out of the question as far as I was concerned because the tub was rather small and because I did not know anything about inflatable birthing tubs at the time.

My Third Birth

Because this was my third delivery, I figured that things would go easier and a lot quicker than they did with my first two babies. Boy was I wrong!

I thought the third birth was going to be a piece of cake; therefore, I decided to wing it and just have the baby on the bed. I did not want to do the water birth this time because of the small tub situation and because I was not in my own home. I was also not comfortable using someone else's tub to bring my baby into the world. Mary did tell me that she could provide an inflatable birthing tub that I could use, but I thought that there would be no need to use that contraption because I was going to be delivering rather quickly. And because I had no idea what a birthing tub was at the time, I really could not picture myself being in an inflatable tub in the middle of the bedroom delivering my baby. I could not get with that image because I had not done any research on what birthing tubs were. All I knew was that I wanted the delivery to go fast and be as painless as possible.

> **"My husband even gave me** those energy boosting gel packs that marathon runners take during a race because delivering a baby is somewhat like running a marathon."

By the time I stepped up the plate to have my third baby, I had heard many stories of women experiencing very smooth and quick deliveries with their third child. I kept telling myself, "You've done this twice before; therefore you are more than prepared to handle this one". Knowing what I know now, I should've taken Mary up on her offer of using the inflatable tub. These inflatable tubs are specifically designed for birthing babies. However, I was not familiar with them because I had never heard of them. Even though Mary explained to me how they worked, I still refused her offer. I guess you can say that I was bit naïve because I thought I could deliver my child the all-natural way…quickly and without pain. Well, that didn't happen.

The day before I went into labor, I had been out and about pretty much all day doing my final errands. At around 2 o'clock that afternoon, I had a strange feeling that I probably shouldn't be driving anymore. So, I went home and decided to call my mother so she could make arrangements to pick up my kids from school. That afternoon, I took things fairly easy, and I told my husband, "I think I'm going to be going into labor pretty soon". Therefore, we decided to put the kids in bed early, hoping that I would go into labor in the early hours of the morning — a time when the kids would still be asleep. It was about 10 o'clock at night that I eventually fell asleep. I started getting a few pains here and there but nothing too strong. At about one in the morning, however, I began to feel much stronger pains. My husband had not slept a wink; he pretty much stayed awake the whole time, keeping track of the timing of my contractions. I would tell him, "Here comes one", and we would then time them from the start of a contractions to the beginning of the next one.

> **"WITH THAT INFORMATION, I knew that I had to deliver the baby without the assistance of any pain killers. There was now no turning back for me."**

My Third Birth

This way we could see a rhythm forming, understanding that the closer they are, the closer you are to giving birth.

Mary instructed me when to call her to come over based upon when my contractions had reached a certain interval. The timing of your contractions is something that you will need to concentrate on when you are in labor. Timing the contractions is something that I did routinely with all my deliveries. But this is a task best assumed by your partner because you will be in too much pain to focus on timing your uterine spasms, which by the way is what contractions are. My husband was great at doing this to the point where he would stay awake and observe me going through each and every contraction I would have. My husband knew that when they were about seven minutes apart, it was time to call Mary to come on over.

So, after about an hour of timing them, my contractions got a lot stronger. By the time I had gotten dressed, my midwife was already there along with one of her students named Amber.

While going through the pains, I couldn't find a comfortable place in the room. It was much harder this time around to simply relax. I could not find any relief from the pain despite my pacing around the room. I did, however, keep up with my fluids. They would give me Gatorade or water with plenty of electrolytes to give me the extra boost of energy I would need later. My husband even gave me those energy boosting gel packs that marathon runners take during a race because delivering a baby is somewhat like running a marathon. During delivery, you need all the energy you can get to stay alert. Therefore, it's important to stay hydrated since you will be losing a lot of liquids.

You will also want to have a good meal before you give birth. During my contractions, Mary would asked me, "When was the last time you ate?" Keep in mind that staying hydrated and eating a good meal are taboo in hospital delivery rooms. They don't want you to be eating or drinking in case you happen to need an emergency C-section. I tend to believe that they are preparing you to undergo that dangerous procedure without you even realizing it. After a few minutes, I finally decided to get on the bed to see if anything would change. I moved around a lot and turned in different ways, but nothing was helping the pain. At least I was able to relax a bit in the warm water with the water births of my first two babies. In the bed, however, I only felt discomfort and pain.

> **"Having fluids and food right away makes a big difference with a woman's recovery."**

At this point, I must be honest. The pain associated with my third delivery was so bad that I even asked Mary if she could give me medication to deal with the labor pains. She simply told me, "It's too late. Besides, you've already gone through the most painful part. Let's just bring the baby out". With that information, I knew that I had to deliver the baby without the assistance of any pain killers. There was now no turning back for me. So, I decided to shift positions and lie on my back and try to push the baby out from that position. While on the bed, I experienced even stronger pains. I was in an awkward position that is typical in a hospital setting. While on my back, I did feel something coming out, and that's when I said to Mary, "Something is out". I discovered quickly that it was only my water that had broken. At this point, I was so excited because it told me that we were one step closer.

Once the water was out, I began having bigger contraction and that's when Mary told me to start slowly pushing and breathing, as I knew to do from the experience of two previous deliveries. Her instructions helped me to push the baby out while remaining calm. A few minutes later, my baby was out. I felt every pain associated with delivering a baby since I was not under any medications. I was completely aware of all the tremendous pain associated with having a baby, and I felt the sensation of the baby slowing exiting my body. Because you experience everything without pain meds, that's what makes these home births such a beautiful experience. As soon as he was out, they placed him on my chest. He was completely covered in a white greasy coating called vernix. This vernix is a thick layer that protects the baby's skin while inside the womb. I was so relieved and thankful to be holding my baby in my arms. I felt a sense of

> "However, according to an article written on the Parent.com website, a bed delivery is the worst way to deliver a baby."

accomplishment, and it felt great. I was so pleased that I had once again DONE IT!

After my baby was born, Mary repeated the same procedures that she performed with my previous two births. The cord was clamped when it stopped pulsing, and it was left attached until I delivered the placenta. Even delivering the placenta was difficult with my third birth because I did not have the assistance of the water to lighten to weight of it all. The one bright spot about the non-water birth is that I was able to stay on the bed and not have to move like I would have had to do had I delivered in the water. My home birth team was able to examine my baby while he was in my arms. Mary did go ahead and inject me with Pitocin to avoid a repeat of the episode during my first delivery where I would not stop bleeding.

> "One of the most important things I learned with my third pregnancy is the importance of maintaining a healthy an active lifestyle all the way up until the delivery date."

I changed out of the cloths that I was wearing during delivery, and they covered me with blankets while my baby was still relaxing on my chest. They performed all the necessary exams on my baby right then and there. He was a perfectly healthy and well developed baby boy. He weighed much less then my previous baby at 7 pounds 3 ounces. My previous baby weighed in at 9 pounds. They continued to give me fluids to stay hydrated, and they even gave me something to eat. Having fluids and food right away makes a big

My Third Birth

difference with a woman's recovery. I remember eating right away, and it felt like I hadn't had food in days. That's how much energy is depleted from your body during child birth. Once again, the ordeal is like running a marathon!

My two kids stayed asleep the whole time while I was in labor. And their room was just a few feet away from mine. When all is said and done, it was a calm and peaceful silent birth. There were about four adults in the room, and we all managed to maintain absolute silence while we introduced our baby boy into the world. My two children in the other room had no idea what was going on because they stayed asleep the entire time. It was about 4 a.m. when the room was finally cleaned up and I was nicely tucked in the bed. We decided to wake the kids up later that morning as if it were Christmas morning to tell them that their baby brother had arrived. They were so shocked and excited that they couldn't believe what they were seeing — that tiny bundle of joy I held snuggly in my arms!

They welcomed the baby with a lot of love and happiness, wanting to hold him right away. Their many questions filled the room. They wanted to know how he came to be. I simply explained that we had him here in the room with Mary who was on hand to help bring him into the world. I skirted around the biological particulars by simply telling them I had him on the bed. But again, they stood suspended in a state of disbelief, trying to wrap their minds around the mystery of it all. Their young eyes saw no evidence of the delivery process that had taken place only a few hours prior because by now the room was nice and neat. Nevertheless, they were thrilled to see their new brother.

When I finally made the call to my mom, I again told her that I didn't make it to the hospital and that I ended up having the baby at home once again. By now, she seemed to be fine with the home birth thing, and I even believe that she got the idea that I had been planning the home births all along. Despite how our new child came into the world, she was thrilled and rushed right over to meet the new bundle of joy.

As with the two others, this third birth went off without a hitch, and there were no scares or worries to speak of. Yet, this one was very tough for me mentally and physically because, in my estimation, I was in a different environment that didn't feel comfortable to me and also because I didn't have a birthing tub to enjoy the relaxing feel of the warm water.

> "LOOKING BACK AT HOW MY third birth unfolded, I now realize that I should have listened to Mary by using the inflatable birthing tub she offered for my use."

Nevertheless, because of the silent birth method that we adhered to, I still enjoyed an overall peaceful and quiet home birth. I really held in my frustrations and kept my calm in tact so that I could experience my third birth in a different way. This bed thing was new to me, and I really didn't know how to lie or how to adjust my body. In hospitals, bed delivery is the only way they want you to have your baby. However, according to an article written on the Parent.com website, a bed delivery is the worst way to deliver a baby. Why? Because there is no gravity to help aid you in the birth of the baby, it compresses all of your major vessels, and you are more likely to have to have an episiotomy due to tearing. Believe it or not, the best positions to deliver a baby are: 1) sitting position, 2) squatting position, 3) moving around, 4) side-lying, and 5) leaning or kneeling forward with support. However, the ultimate posture for birthing a baby is in a tub filled with warm watering.

> "I AM SO GLAD THAT I HAD PASSED the safe threshold and that my midwife did not allow me to take any meds to numb the pain. Who knows how things could have ended up?"

In closing...

One of the most important things I learned with my third pregnancy is the importance of maintaining a healthy an active lifestyle all the way up until the delivery date. But please make sure that your midwife or doctor is aware of the workout regimen you are following in order that he or she can best monitor how the stress of your exercising is affecting you and your baby.

It is also important to keep in mind that you will definitely need to develop a comprehensive birth plan if you have existing children who will be around at the time of your delivery. The plan will ensure that arrangements will be made for someone to take care of your children while you are in the process of bringing another child into the world.

Looking back at how my third birth unfolded, I now realize that I should have listened to Mary by using the inflatable birthing tub she offered for my use. Instead, I chose to deliver my third baby on a bed. But at least I now know the pros and cons of both types of home birthing options. Comparing a water birth to a non-water birth, I can now say without hesitation that delivering a baby in warm water beats all other methods hands down. I am a firm believer that nothing beats a water birth because your overall birthing experience will be so much more relaxing and stress-free. I also learned that there is a narrow window during delivery when it is safe to take pain medication to ease the pain…but beyond which it is not safe to do so. Thinking back on my state of mind at the time, I can't believe I asked for the pain meds. I am so glad that I had passed the safe threshold and that my midwife did not allow me to take any meds to numb the pain. Who knows how things could have ended up?

Chapter Eight
OH, WHAT A SACRIFICE!

My third home birth revealed that I have a high tolerance for pain. It also showed me that a water birth is so much better than a bed birth. I can't stress enough how much more relaxing and relieving to the body it is to be in water when delivering a baby. But there was one thing that surprised me about my third delivery. Because of my adamant position on natural child birth, I can't believe I asked for pain medication to help get me through this particular delivery. After all, my whole purpose for pursuing home births in the first place was to stay away from the pain medications. I just didn't want my babies to suffer from any of their ill-effects. Many women I have spoken to on the matter claim they can't go through labor without some form of pain killer? They point me out and tell me that I'm a rare, brave woman to be able to deliver a baby without the use of pain relief medication.

Nowadays, there is such a strong push on the part of the healthcare industry to get mothers to simply take the easy route by receiving pain relief medicine during delivery because it helps to get women in and out quicker. Prior to me ever getting pregnant, I didn't know much about the pros and cons of the various pain relief medications used for child birth. The only thing I knew was that it kept women from feeling pain while in labor and during delivery. But what risks do these pain killers pose to the health of the babies? And why is it that so many women today can't seem to endure the delivery process without the need for pain relief drugs? I have personally experienced three home births without the desire to reach for an epidural or any other type of pain management. In fact, I went through the discomfort of having a nine pound baby in water and a seven pound baby without the aid of water — both delivery methods took place at home without the assistance of medication of any kind. I don't want to condemn any woman who feels she needs it, but I simply wish to let you know that you can get through the ordeal of labor without pain medication and also to give you an idea of what it is like to go through labor without any pain relievers.

> **"Giving birth to my children without medication was one sacrifice I felt compelled to make."**

Birthing Without Anesthesia: Why Sacrifice?

As a mother, you will go through a great many sacrifices for the sake of your children — from the time when they are newborns until the point when they leave your nest and beyond. Giving birth to my children without medication was one sacrifice I felt compelled to make. My initial research into the home birth option was so that I could avoid exposure to the healthcare industry medications. I didn't want my babies exposed to any drugs. Whether the epidural even reaches the baby or not, I just wanted to make sure that I did not expose my child to any type of medications that could adversely affect them. My search for drug-free birthing methods led me to realize that when a woman gets an epidural that some of that medication ends up in the baby's system; therefore, the delivery team needs to flush the medicine out of the baby. So, in order for them to do that, they give the baby sugar water to detox the baby from any drugs that they may have been exposed to. This procedure is a fact that was revealed in the documentary "The Business of Being Born". It was this very documentary that influenced me to have a home birth.

> **"THE SUGAR GIVEN TO your baby fills him up and delays his nursing instincts."**

Of course, the hospitals won't tell you any of this because to do so would affect their bottom-line. They just bring your baby back to you after a few hours, and you realize your baby is not hungry. Geeze, I wonder why? After all, they just filled your baby's little belly with sugar water. Now you have another situation to deal with. The sugar given to your baby fills him up and delays his nursing instincts. Therefore, the natural bonding process that should take place between mother and baby through breast feeding is delayed because the baby is not hungry by the time he is brought to the mother. That is why I chose to avoid all of that by having a home birth.

Over the years, I have had many women ask me all kinds of questions about child birth. Once they realize that I did it the natural way without medication, they wanted to know more. They wanted to know how it was possible to go through the pain of delivery without medication. So, I wanted to let them know what they would feel while going through labor without pain relief medication. Every birth is different; therefore, the level of pain associated with each delivery will be different, as well. However, I can give you an idea of the pain I felt and pressed through so that you can know that you too can get through the discomfort of your labor and delivery.

> "**These false flags don't cause** labor, but they can be very uncomfortable. They are pretty much preparing the body for labor."

When you are about 4-5 months pregnant, you will begin to experience a sensation known as Braxton Hicks contractions, and they are considered to be "false" or "practice" contractions. Some women don't feel them at all until they are about to start actual labor. But if you do, these false contractions feel like mild menstrual cramps. Some women describe them as a feeling of tightening in the abdomen that comes and goes. These false flags don't cause labor, but they can be very uncomfortable. They are pretty much preparing the body for labor. I tend to think of them as the advance guard, which is gearing you up for the actual labor yet to come. So you see, this is what you will be feeling. This is the pain that you have to go through in order for you to have a natural birth. Indeed, the pain will increase, but you have to keep in mind that it will come and go. The pain won't last forever. It will go away! And in the end, you will get to embrace the reward you have been waiting nine months to dote over. That is why I believe that having a baby is sixty percent mental and forty percent physical. Take these Braxton Hicks contractions as mental preparation for what is to come later.

> **"THAT IS WHY I BELIEVE THAT** having a baby is sixty percent mental and forty percent physical."

When your actual labor starts, it will feel like Braxton Hicks contractions. As the labor pains get closer, they will intensify, and the pain will get harder to deal with. Labor pains are very painful, but the wave-like spasms in the uterus come and go like the ebb and flow of an ocean tide. When you are in real labor, the pain you feel in the uterine region is called contractions. The pain results from the tightening of the abdomen and the opening of the cervix to prepare that area so the baby can come out. Whenever I would experience my contractions, I would simply tell myself that each one was getting me one step closer to seeing my baby. That mental game helped me to deal with the pains of child birth. So, the closer you get to labor, the more intense these contractions will get.

What also helped me deal with painful contractions was tightly gripping something, anything — whether someone's hand or a bed rail. I would simply walk around until I found a spot where I could grab something. I would also wear a mouth guard to protect my teeth against the damage that could result from tight clenching. My contractions would last anywhere from half a minute to one minute with the onset of each episode, and I would have anywhere from about three to thirty minutes to catch my breath. The intervening breaks would get progressively shorter and shorter over time, which means you will get to breathe a sigh of relief less frequently as your labor pains get closer and closer in frequency. The closer the contractions are, the nearer you are to delivering your baby. Please keep in mind that you should use the break periods wisely. At least, that's how I took advantage of those precious moments of peace and calm. I would drink Gatorade or some type of energy drinks.

> "**Not having an epidural** speeds the labor process because it doesn't numb your body or put you to sleep."

While in the tub during a water birth, I could easily shift my body to best handle the contractions as they came. The pain of the contractions feels a lot like severe stomach pains, but ten times more intense. But again the pain will go away. You have to keep telling yourself that the pain is but a momentary sacrifice that you are making for your baby. An important point to remember is that when no epidural is introduced into the equation, a typical delivery takes on average between two to three hours from the point of the first contraction to the moment when the baby is fully delivered. Some women are in labor for hours, but mainly due to the effects of an epidural. Not having an epidural speeds the labor process because it doesn't numb your body or put you to sleep.

Once your baby is delivered, the pain goes away rather quickly. You will feel sore, like you had the hardest workout ever. If you've ever had a strenuous workout where you gave your arms, legs and back a serious burn, that's how you will feel after delivery. In reality, delivering a baby is more grueling on the body than any workout you will ever get in a gym. But you will feel better with each passing day as your body continues to heal and recover.

> "**AND IF YOUR RESEARCH LEAVES** you feeling rather uneasy, then a medication-free delivery just may be the first huge sacrifice you decide to make on behalf of your baby."

So, just keep in the back of your mind during the early stages of your pregnancy that the false indications are merely Braxton Hicks contractions. They will, however, give you a taste of what your actual labor pains will feel like. They can also give you a pretty good indicator of your pain threshold. Now if you can't go through the Braxton Hicks contractions without the need for pain relief medication, then you may want to consider incorporating the pain medication option. But I would strongly recommend that you do your research on the side effects of pain meds and how they can affect your baby. And if your research leaves you feeling rather uneasy, then a medication-free delivery just may be the first huge sacrifice you decide to make on behalf of your baby.

Water Breaking

With all of my home births, my water broke while I was in labor, which is typical. It is normal for a woman's water to break at the beginning of or during labor. Although, there are many women who experience rupture to the amniotic sac before labor even starts. This is known as premature rupture of membranes or PROM. Needless to say, this just goes to show that every labor is different. Without anesthesia to lessen the pain, you will feel just about everything that comes out of your body. You will be fully aware of every sensation taking place within. With my first birth, I had no idea what sensations I would feel in my body, let alone what fluids I would be releasing during labor. But when I was sitting in a warm bath tub going through a bout of contractions, I did feel something flowing out of me. I remember telling someone that I felt something being excreted out of me that I could not control. It was a weird feeling because I could not keep inside what so desperately wanted to escape. I soon discovered that my amniotic sac had ruptured. In other words, my water had broken.

With the delivery of my third baby, however, my water broke in the middle of labor while I was on the bed. Again, I felt that same strange feeling that I couldn't control. But this time, water was all over the bed. Every time I felt my water come out, I knew I was closer to delivering my baby. Though the sensation was weird, I wanted to have the presence of mind to experience every feeling and not be cheated out of the moment by being drugged up. I couldn't imagine being in a groggy state while going through labor. I wanted to be mentally alert and fully engaged. The minute I felt that my water had broken, I knew I was close to delivering my baby and that I should start pushing. When my contractions were coming and going, I felt an instinctual urge to start pushing. However, I followed my midwife instructions regarding when I should and should not push. After only a few pushes, I felt the head trying to come out. Following her directions, I pushed until the baby was fully out. All said and done, it took me only a few pushes to deliver my baby. When I say that you will feel everything, trust me, you will feel everything — from the time your baby's head first appears to the moment he or she is exiting the vaginal cavity. It's quite a relief to feel the baby finally exit your body. I had all kinds of emotions come over me the moment the ordeal had ended and I held my baby for the first time. Yes, it is very painful when the baby is actually coming out, but the pain quickly goes away as soon as you see and hold your precious bundle of joy.

> **"I HAD ALL KINDS OF EMOTIONS** come over me the moment the ordeal had ended and I held my baby for the first time."

You will definitely want to be fully aware of everything that goes on during your delivery. I can't stress enough that you don't want to be in a situation where you are not fully awake or you are too sedated to fully focus on what is taking place while you are delivering your baby. But if you have an epidural, you may feel dull, groggy, and even a little high from the anesthesia injected into your lower spine. It's not fully known what the long term effects are to a woman's body, or the baby's for that matter. I have heard some women say that they can't feel their legs or their abdomen behind getting an epidural. But having leg and abdomen sensation is vital to a woman's ability to push during contractions. Being fully aware gives you the ability to be in the driver's seat when it comes to birthing your baby.

> "WHILE I WAS WAITING FOR THE placenta to come out, I held my baby in my arms the whole time, all the while the baby was still attached to the placenta."

BIRTHING THE PLACENTA

Now after you have delivered your baby, you will now need to push out the placenta. When I first realized that I had yet another major task to perform, I was in shock. I told my midwife, "You have got to be kidding me". I literally thought I would have to endure that pain all over again. But the reality is the hard part is behind you. When it's time for the placenta to be delivered, you will experience only mild contractions that follow, but nothing at all like when you were pushing your baby out. You will feel a mild tightening of the abdomen. These small contractions occur in order to expel the placenta. This usually takes anywhere between five to thirty minutes after you have delivered your baby. These spasms are not painful, but they can be uncomfortable based upon the size of the placenta that needs to come out.

My midwife was by my side to assist me in delivering the placenta. I can remember being in the tub waiting for the contractions to start, and I would get a sudden urge to start pushing the placenta. While I was waiting for the placenta to come out, I held my baby in my arms the whole time, all the while the baby was still attached to the placenta. Once the placenta was out, then my midwife placed it in a container so they could examine it to make sure it was fully intact, with nothing left behind. I have never had pieces of my placenta break off and remain inside of me. If this should occur, however, there are steps your midwife is prepared to take to remove them, as this can cause other complications. Once you have done the hard part of pushing your baby out, delivering the placenta is really small potatoes? Delivering the placenta usually happens so quickly that you might not even notice when it occurs because you typically will be so preoccupied with holding your baby that you might not even notice the process. I didn't pay much attention to when I delivered the placenta after having my first baby because it was rather quick and painless.

> **"Once you have done the hard part of pushing your baby out, delivering the placenta is really small potatoes?"**

In closing...

What To Expect From Your Home Birthing Experience

There are so many benefits to being able to deliver a baby in a medication-free, clear state of mind. When you are not drugged up, you can make decisions that are in the best interest of you and your baby. And you remain in complete control of how you want things to go when you are in labor. Having an epidural or any other pain relief medication can certainly leave you feeling groggy and out of it. While these drugs can ease the pain, they will most likely leave you with hazy recollections of your delivery, and you don't want that. I am very proud to say that I delivered all four of my children without the assistance of pain meds. I know that you too are capable of having a natural birth without the use of drugs. So, when they tell me that I am brave and strong, I assure them that they are just as capable as I am to bring a child into this world without the use of pain medication. But you must remind yourself that the pain will go away as soon as your baby is born and you get to hold her. And you must also remind yourself of the importance of the sacrifice you are making so that your child will have a chance at the healthiest start in life. After all, this natural way of giving birth is how women have done it since the dawn of man — before the advent of modern medicine. And you can too!

Chapter Nine
MY SWAN SONG

When I started writing this book, I was expecting my fourth and final baby. After much thought, my husband and I decided to make a final go at it, since we didn't feel our family was complete. For starters, I wanted a girl because I already had one girl and two boys. But even though I may have wanted another child, I felt from the start that I was not ready to undergo another delivery. In all honestly, I wished that I didn't have to go through the pain of child birth. But in all truth, the pain of delivery is part of the inevitable sacrifice that every mother must make. Again, I was very fortunate to have Mary on hand for my swan song delivery. She was more than willing to be by my side one last time.

By this point, our situation had changed a bit. We were finally in our new home, and we were delighted to have at least one of our kids born in an environment that was ours. This birth, however, was one I was not fully prepared for. Fortunately, though, everything went well despite the fact that things were different in many ways.

I Am Truly Done This Time!

I know that I am not alone when I talk about the feeling a woman has when she knows she is done having more children. I also hear so many women speak about the regret they feel behind closing shop and ruling out the possibility of having another baby. And then too there are those women who have had to make major adjustments to their lives in order to welcome into this world a surprise baby! I felt that it was important for me to pay close attention to all the different "baby having" or "baby not having" scenarios. Was I truly done after my third baby? I always knew I wanted at least three kids. However, after having my third baby, I never felt like I was complete. I can recall asking certain women who were done with the baby-making thing, "When did you get that feeling that you didn't want more children, and what did it fell like?"

> "**Apparently some women feel** a huge sense of fulfillment when they have achieved having a certain number of children and no longer have a maternal desire for more."

Apparently some women feel a huge sense of fulfillment when they have achieved having a certain number of children

My Swan Song

and no longer have a maternal desire for more. They know deep from within that they are done and that they are content with the idea of shutting down the factory for good. After my third child, I wasn't feeling like I was complete. All I can remember is that I wanted another baby. I was left with the profound sense of knowing that I'm going to miss changing diapers. I also felt tremendous sadness at the fact that this would be the last baby I would ever nurse. Once my son was out of diapers, I felt a certain melancholy mood engulf me as I pondered not be able to change anymore diapers. This sadness continued to swell with every stage of my son's growth and development. These feelings were a first for me, and I was not at all happy about having to face them.

> "Once my son was out of diapers, I felt a certain melancholy mood engulf me as I pondered not be able to change anymore diapers."

As someone who is always eager to learn more, I would bluntly ask women, "When did you get the feeling that you didn't want any more children?" I so desperately needed to experience this feeling for myself so that I could know definitively when I was done them. I could not picture myself not having any more children. When I did, a sad feeling would overwhelm me. After child number three, I never felt that I was completely done, so my husband and I decided we would do the home birth thing one more time and call it quits at child number four. So, after I got pregnant and went through nine months of pregnancy, it was slowly dawning on me that this would be my last pregnancy. I felt satisfied with the decision my husband and I had made. This feeling that some women get of not needing to have any more children can come at any moment. I believe that when you are done having children, and I mean truly done, you won't be saddened at the thought of that anymore. Instead, it will be a chapter of life that you will begin to look forward to.

After having my fourth baby, I felt complete. I think the feeling of fulfillment hit me as soon as she was born. Holding her in my arms, I pondered the fact that she would be my last home birth, and I was now content with that reality. I felt that we were now complete as a family and that I could close this chapter in my life. Had I not had my fourth child, I would have been left with a void in my life that nothing else could have filled. I point this out because there are so many women who feel the same way I did. They are left to wonder, "Should we go for another baby, or are we really done?" You have to have a serious conversation with your husband or partner and decide whether the two of you are done having children. I am so happy my husband and I had the talk because we are now complete as a family.

> "Had I not had my fourth child, I would have been left with a void in my life that nothing else could have filled."

My Final Pregnancy

Given that this was my fourth and final pregnancy, I had a

good idea how I wanted to approach it. I wanted to continue pursuing a healthy lifestyle like I had done with my third pregnancy, and I wanted to continue taking my vitamin supplements. I was very fortunate in that I did not experience any morning sickness with any of my pregnancies, and I also never experienced any nausea that is typically associated with pregnancy. I did, however, experience plenty of fatigue and sleepiness. Keep in mind that I still had three other children at home to care for. I was fortunate also to have Mary by my side throughout my fourth pregnancy, as she had been during my three previous home births. This time, however, she brought with her several students whom she was training in midwifery. These students were very helpful. I was happy to know that her work was being replicated by others. Mary conducted my appointments at my home, and by now, I was pretty familiar with the entire labor and delivery process. I continued to be seen by the same ob-gyn who had monitored my previous two births, recalling that he was the doctor who did not oppose my home births; although, he respectfully advised against them.

> **"This final time around, my ob-gyn appointments felt more like mere perfunctory rituals than anything else."**

This final time around, my ob-gyn appointments felt more like mere perfunctory rituals than anything else. My visits were something that I did simply to have a backup option in the event that an emergency occurred with my home birth. In reality, I didn't even need them because they lacked significance when viewed in light of my home birth plan. Seeing my midwife for my appointments was sufficient enough for me and my baby. In fact, her appointments were more thorough, and they were just as accurate as my ob-gyn's assessments. But again, I simply kept the ob-gyn appointments for my own peace of mind — not out of necessity because at the end of the day, I knew that he would not be delivering my baby.

Baby is Ready...I am Not!

It was two days before my actual due date. Therefore, I was not expecting anything to happen. I did not feel ready to have the baby. In fact, throughout this entire pregnancy, I never felt ready to have the baby — not mentally and certainly not physically. I did not want to go through labor pains again. I was hoping to have a quick delivery with the baby just slipping out painlessly. According to my midwife, my thoughts were normal and common. The morning of my delivery was as typical as any other day. I woke up and felt normal and energized. I showered and got ready to face the day. I planned to spend the morning with my kids at their school. However, at about 7 a.m. that morning, I started to feel a few small contractions, but I figured that they would soon go away. I continued getting the kids ready for school and making breakfast when, all of as sudden, another contraction started. I

> "I HAD THIS STRANGE FEELING that maybe he shouldn't leave and that I should let him know what was happening with me."

quickly dismissed the significance of that episode and concluded that that single contraction would be the end of them. But it wasn't to be that way.

They continued to mount their attack, growing stronger with each new assault. I didn't mention anything to my husband about the battle that had already begun because he was already on his way out the door headed for work. I had this strange feeling that maybe he shouldn't leave and that I should let him know what was happening with me. But I didn't say anything because I wanted the pains to stop coming and just go away. He did in fact leave for work, and all I could do is watch the door close behind him. So, when it was time for me and the kids to leave for school, I decided that it would be better to have a friend come by and take them to school for me because the pains kept coming, and there was no way for me to drive in my condition.

> **"I FIBBED BY TELLING MARY** that I was experiencing mild contractions because I was not ready to deliver a baby today."

Once I was home alone, I started walking around the house and timing my contractions. My first thought was to call Mary, but I didn't want to do this today because I was not ready. I hesitated to call her. So, I just stared at my phone. I finally got my cell phone and looked up her number. But again, the only thing I could do was stare at it. I couldn't believe I was doing this today. Part of me didn't want to do this because I simply didn't want to feel the pain. But the contractions kept coming, and they were a little stronger each time. It was about 8 a.m. when I finally decided to call her. I tried to appear nonchalant by asking Mary if she had performed any deliveries this morning and inquiring as to how she was doing. I knew she had a few back-to-back deliveries this week — me being one of them. She stated that she was just thinking about me and that I was next on her schedule. She indicated that she was concerned that I hadn't called her earlier in the week.

I fibbed by telling Mary that I was experiencing mild contractions because I was not ready to deliver a baby today. She told me to call her in 15 minutes if anything changes or if the contractions became more intense and closer together. With those instructions, I agreed to call her back. After getting off the phone with Mary, I decided to let my husband know what was going on. When I attempted to call him on his cell phone, it went straight to voicemail. My first thought was that he had no charge on his phone. Nevertheless, I kept trying to reach him on his phone, but to no avail.

> **"AT THAT MOMENT, IT FINALLY** dawned on me that I needed to prepare myself for a birth because those contractions were not going anywhere."

Instead, I decided to call his office number, but the receptionist told me that he was busy. She asked me if it was an emergency, stating that she would interrupt him if it was. After hesitating for what seemed like minutes, I told her not to bother him but to have him call me when he had a free moment.

By that time, the fifteen minutes had elapsed and I failed to call Mary back to tell her that indeed they were getting closer and more intense. Instead, she called me back and asked me how I was doing. At that moment, it finally dawned on me that I needed to prepare myself for a birth because those contractions were not going anywhere. She told me she was on her way over to my home, and she asked if my husband was there. To which, I told her no, I'm home alone. When I hung up the phone with her, I decided to change into something more comfortable. My husband finally called from work, and I worked up the courage to tell him about my contractions. "This is it", I said, "We will be having a baby here soon." He quickly hung up the phone and headed straight home.

While waiting for Mary, the friend who had helped me with the kids arrived and asked if she could be of any help. By now it was about 8:30 in the morning, and my contractions were stronger and more painful. I kept trying to walk around and get a hold of things to help me through each contraction. I saw the tub in the restroom and thought, "I don't think I'm going to make it in time to use it." However, I did tell her to help me by filling it with warm water. Amber, who was another Midwife who assisted in the delivery of my third baby, also arrived by this time. She was on hand to assist Mary once more. She showed up before Mary, and she immediately set about assisting me. Right away, she got familiar with the space she would be working in, and she began filling the inflatable tub. She also indicated that she didn't believe I would get to use the tub since my contractions were stronger and closer together by now. I told her that my husband was on his way and that Mary should be here any minute now.

Because my baby was so close to coming out, she told me to get on the bed with my knees and hands on the bed and with my head towards my chest. She indicated that this position slows down the contractions and holds the baby in its current position. While on the bed, I watched as the tub filled in what seemed like slow motion, and my thoughts were constantly on the fact that my husband had not arrived home yet. Fortunately, Mary arrived and saw the position I was in. My husband finally arrived around 9:15 a.m. to see me on the bed in that strange position. He immediately comes to my side and tells me that he's excited to be having our last baby. As I grip my husband's hand, I calmly go through that next round of contractions while the tub is still being filled with warm water.

> "While on the bed, I watched as the tub filled in what seemed like slow motion, and my thoughts were constantly on the fact that my husband had not arrived home yet."

All the while, Mary and Amber are busy preparing the room for child birth. Within myself, I'm wondering whether the tub is going to be ready for me to use. I feel that it's taking way too long to fill with water. I keep asking, "Is it ready yet?", and the only reply I got was, "No, almost!" By now, I'm hesitant to use the tub because I don't think it will be ready in time. I ask Mary if I should still get in, and she assures me that it will be ready for me to use. We keep the room lights off and close the curtains so it stays dark and quiet. At last, she directs me to get into the tub. I try to move as quickly as I can during a break between contractions. While in the tub, the water continues to fill to a comfortable level. The warm water hits my body, and it instantly relaxes me. As I look around the room, I see the friend who helped me earlier in the morning with my children. But in that moment, I told my husband to have her leave the room, as I was not comfortable having her there. I wanted to make sure that the only people in the room this morning were my familiar home birth comrades. My husband asked her in a polite way to leave the room, and she did.

> **"I STARTED GETTING A LITTLE** impatient since I didn't feel or see any signs of the baby coming. Mary told me to just concentrate, and let's just bring her down slowly."

By now, it was about 9:30 a.m., and I was simply trying to calm myself and get through each contraction. My husband stayed close by just holding my hand while I was going through the labor pains. Amber tried to get a heartbeat with the monitor submerged in the water, but every time she went to listen to the heartbeat, a contraction came on. So, she stopped and waited for it to pass. While I am in the tub, I noticed that my stomach had not dropped and that my water had not broken. I started getting a little impatient since I didn't feel or see any signs of the baby coming. Mary told me to just concentrate, and let's just bring her down slowly. All of a sudden, I got a strong, deep contraction that seemed to be longer than usual, and I felt my water break. And I could also feel the baby coming down, as well. Mary told me that her head is out. I realized that if I could muster one more push, she would be completely out. Therefore, I held my breath, and I pushed. Voila! Out she came. It felt so good to push and feel her finally come out. She started crying very loudly, and I felt relieved and grateful.

They placed her on my chest and put warm towels on her. She was born at around 10 a.m. I spent about 30 minutes in water, which was a shorter time than it took them to fill the tub. I was glad to have gotten in the warm water because I felt less pain when it was time to push. All that time, I was so afraid of feeling the delivery pains that I tried to avoid the entire delivery all together. In the end, the pains were not as bad as I was fearing, and they turned out to be very manageable. The water did make a big difference when it came to the intensity of the pain. This time around, my delivery was shorter than with my previous births. Although my average time in the delivery process is about 3-hours total, I feel this one was less than two hours.

> **"IT IS TYPICALLY HARMLESS TO** newborns, except in cases when they inhale it into the lungs. Then it can become potentially life-threatening for the baby.**"**

UNUSUAL OUTCOME

I stayed in the water for another 20 minutes so I could birth the placenta. I held my baby while they give her a quick check and to suction the amniotic fluid from her nose, mouth, and throat. They then exchanged the dirty, wet towels with clean, dry ones and kept her on my chest. Once the placenta was out, I got up out of the tub, changed into dry clothes, and moved to the bed. I handed the baby to my husband so I could make the transition. My body felt sore and heavy. As I motioned to get myself out of the water, I felt very weak all of a sudden. The midwives helped me out of the tub and quickly laid me on the bed. They gave me fluids to replace lost electrolytes, and they fought to keep me awake. The movement of me getting up after the stress of labor weakened me and left me feeling dizzy. Once on my bed, I felt so much better. I was able to change into a clean gown and dry off a bit.

> "FINALLY, MARY BRINGS ME up to seed with the small scare once she is certain there's no need to worry."

The baby stayed attached to the placenta while the midwives examined her. She looked so content and peaceful. Mary told me that they wanted to examine her right away since they noticed the presence of meconium, which is the first feces of a newborn. It is typically harmless to newborns, except in cases when they inhale it into the lungs. Then it can become potentially life-threatening for the baby. The condition is known as meconium aspiration syndrome (MAS). The meconium is dark, thick and sticky, but it has no smell to it. The sight of meconium is a sign of fetal distress. The detection of meconium in labor can cause suffocation to the baby. I never experienced this with any of my other births;

although, I had heard about it prior to the births of my children. But never had I ever been a firsthand witnessed of MAS.

When she had come out and was in my arms, I noticed something dark that was on her. It was a very small amount, but it was something I had never seen before. Mary was very confident that it was nothing to be concerned about, but she wanted to take every precaution by checking her thoroughly. Normally, they would check the babies the next day or a few hours after birth. This time, however, they checked my baby within the first hour she was born, and it was a very thorough check up. The placenta was still attached while they were examining her. This was an amazing sight to see — the baby lying on the bed while still attached to the placenta. This just goes to show how remarkable life is — how our bodies are created to sustain another life. Mary saw no sign of trouble, and she concluded that she must have defecated as she was coming out of the womb. The midwives didn't think the baby inhaled any of the meconium either.

> I AM SO DELIGHTED THAT I followed my instincts and had a fourth child. I will never regret making this decision.

Mary mentioned none of this to me until they were done with the baby's exam. So, I had no idea why they were checking her so soon after the delivery. I thought they wanted to perform the examination since my baby was so calm throughout the entire delivery. Finally, Mary brings me up to speed with the small scare once she is certain there's no need to worry. All the tests showed that she was in good health. I am so glad Mary chose to give me the news only after she knew my baby was out of harm's way because I think I would have panicked had I known beforehand. The last thing you want to hear after giving birth is that something went wrong. All you want to hear is that your baby is in good health, which was the case with my baby.

In closing...

After going through my fourth and final delivery, I now feel complete. I was blessed to have successfully delivered two boys and two girls, and all of them in a home setting. Giving birth to my children at home is the best decision I have ever made. I am so delighted that I followed my instincts and had a fourth child. I will never regret making this decision. On the other hand, if I had not followed through with that deep-seated feeling to have just one more child, I think I would have lived with regret the rest of my life.

My pregnancy went as smoothly as can be expected, and I remained in a healthy condition, which helps a lot with your postpartum recovery. As long as you stay active and eat healthy, the chances are great that you will have a healthy baby. Don't try to eat for two during your pregnancy. Eating healthy, balanced meals for yourself is all you need to do.

My final home birth was bitter sweet. I could not have

asked for a smoother or faster delivery than what I experienced. To top things off, I did not experience anywhere near the amount of pain I was anticipating. My initial reluctance and hesitation to acknowledge my labor signs were more as a result of the fear of the pain I was anticipating, which did not manifest. But again, having the warm water really helped with relieving the stress of delivery. To be truthful, I was more worried about delivering my baby without my husband by my side since everything was moving faster than any delivery I had ever experienced. But when you choose to go natural and wait till the baby is ready, then things tend to go much smoother and faster. That's the beauty of home birth. You get to decide how things go. You are in the driver's seat. The best decision I could have made was to have a home birth.

I wholeheartedly stand by every one of my decisions to give birth naturally from the comfort of home. And I unequivocally recommend the home birth option to you, as well.

Conclusion
APPRECIATION FOR THE PROCESS

Several years ago, I set out on a journey to discover the healthiest options available to bring my first child into the world. After an exhaustive search, the home birth solution kept appearing on the radar as the best choice for me. I wrote this book to inform women that there is an alternative outside of the traditional healthcare industry to bring life into the world. Furthermore, I hope also to shed light on the many benefits associated with natural child birth. With each of my four home births, I learned something new — things that no one ever talks about. This book is the culmination of my attempt to encapsulate my experiences for the benefit of other women.

I actually did it…four times over. I defied conventional wisdom and challenged deeply entrenched social norms by giving birth at home under the care of a midwife. And I was able to do it all drug-free. In chapter one I laid out the case for home births by discussing the many benefits of giving birth in the comfort of your own home. In chapter two, we looked at

Conclusion

the role of a midwife and the investigative work needed to identify the right midwife to team up with. We also discussed the difference between a midwife and an ob-gyn.

Believing that sharing my actual experiences is important in answering the many questions women have regarding natural delivery, I included the amazing and sometimes gory details of my actual four deliveries in chapters three, five, seven, and nine. In these chapters, I explained the details of what occurred as well as what I learned from those delivery experiences.

In chapter four I discussed a personal favorite of mine, although it is not a must for having your baby the natural way. In that section, I talked about silent births — what it is and the benefits to your baby. Chapter six tends to fascinate most readers because of the amount of revelatory information it reveals regarding the importance of the umbilical cord and the placenta. This particular chapters takes a look at why Mary chose to delay clamping the umbilical cord until the last possible moment, all the while keeping each of my babies attached to the placentas. Finally, in chapter eight, I discussed the sacrifice I made by delivering an oversized baby without the aid of pain medication.

Observing all of my children, I noticed the closeness and love they have for each other. I attribute this mainly to the fact that they all came into the world through a peaceful home

Conclusion

birth. They deeply love and care for one another in ways that most young siblings don't exhibit. My children never displayed any signs of jealousy at the intrusion of a new baby into the family. Because I gave birth at home, my kids never had to experience me coming home from the hospital a few days later with some strange family addition. They simply went to bed one evening and woke up the next morning to the announcement that a new baby had arrived. I believe, therefore, that when your baby is added to your family by being born right there in the home, this dynamic leaves very little room for jealousy, confusion, and anger. I noticed that when the newborn would cry, each one of my children felt a genuine concern and wanted to help out in some way. They wanted the baby's needs tended to immediately. This is proof positive that a home birth creates a strong, loving bond within the family unit.

It has been a distinct honor and privilege to take this journey with you. I trust that the information I have shared in this book has convinced you that you too can safely deliver your baby naturally from the comfort and convenience of home. If what I have shared between the pages of this book has not caused you to want to take the leap completely, I hope that I have at least caused you to begin thinking about the possibilities of pursuing the home birth option.

Here's to your courage to venture where few dare consider!

Appendix
FREQUENTLY ASKED QUESTION

WHERE DO YOU GO TO FIND A MIDWIFE?

I would recommend looking at local birthing centers in your area or asking friends and family.

IS A BIRTHING CENTER AND HOME BIRTH SIMILAR?

Yes, they are both very similar in that the objective of both birthing methods is to give mom the most natural child birth experience possible. The difference exists with the amount of total privacy you are seeking as a delivering mom. In a home birth environment, you have complete control over your environment. While birthing centers go to great lengths to create an at-home feel with their private rooms, the actual intimacy of being in your own home can never be achieved in birthing center. But keep in mind that the midwife and wellness model are the goal of birthing centers, as much as they are the objective of home births.

WHAT DO YOU WEAR WHEN YOU ARE IN A WATER TUBE?

A simple sports bra or short gown that can get wet. There is really no right attire for what you should wear, as long as you are comfortable.

What does a contraction feel it?

Contractions fell much like severe stomach aches that get progressively more intense in terms of pain level the closer the baby is to being delivered.

How can you manage the pain of contractions?

One of the best ways to deal with contractions is by finding a relaxing environment. Moving constantly also helps to ease the pain, and for that matter, many expecting moms find tremendous relief by walking as much as possible during the contraction episodes. You may also find relief by taking a warm shower or bath. Finally, I would recommend that you find something that you can grab firmly. This really helped me a lot during my hour of need.

Where can you find an inflatable tub?

Your midwife should be able to find one for you or recommend a retailer, or you can do an internet search for a retailer.

Do you recommend having siblings in the room while you are birthing?

My kids were not present during any of my home births because I wanted it to be a private moment between me and my baby. However, if you feel comfortable with your children in the room, then by all means, allow them to enjoy the special moment.

Appendix

Is pain management an available option with a home birth?

My midwife assured me that pain management drugs were an option she kept on hand during all of my four births. I, however, chose to deliver all of my babies without that the assistance of pain relief medication. But this is something that you would need to discuss with your midwife.

Is Deming the lights a good option?

Absolutely! It creates a calm environment and relaxes you by creating a spa like feeling.

Is a silent birth a common practice among midwives?

No, it is not. In fact, my midwife had never heard about the concept until I introduced it to her. As mentioned in the book, I first ran across the silent birth concept by reading some of L. Ron Hubbard's ideas about child birth. But I can tell you that all four of my kids are very happy and calm children to this day. They love and care for each other. And I attribute much of the similarities in their personalities to all of them experiencing a silent birth.

Who does the placenta encapsulation for you?

The same midwife who delivered my baby did it for me. This is one question that your midwife can help you with.

What were some of the benefits from encapsulating the placenta?

It helped with my energy levels. I feel that it helped me with restoring my figure to its pre-pregnancy form and with losing the weight faster than would otherwise have been the case. It also helped increase my milk production.

ABOUT HOW MANY PILLS DO YOU GET FROM THE PLACENTA?

It depends on the size of the placenta you have to begin with. However, I was able to get about a 3-month supply of capsules each time I did placenta encapsulation.

IS BREASTFEEDING THE BEST OPTION?

Indeed it is. Not only is it very convenient for the mother to use her own milk to feed her baby, but breast milk is far healthier and more nutrient-rich than commercially manufactured infant formula brands.

DOES BREASTFEEDING COME EASY THE SECOND OR THIRD TIME AROUND?

Yes, because you already know how to latch the baby to your breast for optimal feeding. However, it is also more painful than the first time around. In the beginning, the pain can be intense, but within a few days the discomfort diminishes significantly. Given that breastfeeding is the healthiest option for your baby, it is so worth it to breastfeed.

DID I EVER USE FORMULA?

No, I was able to nurse all my babies for one full year on my breast milk. After that, I introduced them to goat's milk. Goat milk is easier to digest than cow's milk. But at about 18 months of age, I switched them over to cow's milk.

Appendix

WHAT IS THE ONE GOOD OUTCOME FROM HAVING A HOME BIRTH I HAVE OBSERVED ONCE THE BABY IS BORN?

All four of my children are very well-adjusted individuals. And I attribute this to the very peaceful home environment into which they were born. None of my children were exposed to the heavy mix of drugs commonly exposed to moms and newborns in hospital delivery units. As a result, my children rarely get sick, as they all have very robust immune systems.

Published by:
Bella Bach Publishing

ISBN: 978-1-7334982-0-3

$14.95

www.ingramcontent.com/pod-product-compliance
Lightning Source LLC
Chambersburg PA
CBHW052051070526
44584CB00017B/2124